WHOLE: 100 WHOLE FOOD RECIPES FOR HEALTH AND WEIGHT LOSS

30 Day Whole Food Challenge Cookbook with 100 AWARD WINNING Whole Food Diet Recipes

By Albert Pino

Legal notice

Join Albert Pino's VIP Club

Get access to exclusive content from Albert including healthy living tips, tricks and hacks, special discounts, recipes, and free books!

www.albertpino.com

TABLE OF CONTENTS

WHOLE FOOD DINNER RECIPES.....................132

THE WHOLE FOOD DIET

Perhaps the single most important thing to say about the whole food diet is that it isn't really a "diet" at all, or at least not in the way people typically use that word. When we talk about diets, we are often referring to something that is restrictive, unpleasant, and also temporary. In modern times we have come to use dieting as a means to an end. We want to lose weight or improve our health, and so to achieve that goal we are willing to suffer for some short period of time.

There are many problems with this approach. First of all, the concept of dieting as a temporary means to an end results in the so called "yo-yo" affect. This occurs when dieters lose weight while dieting but then immediately gain back all of the weight (and sometimes even more!) after ending their diet regimen.

The second problem is that dieting is typically oriented less around promoting health and more around a particular outcome relating to weight loss or something more superficial than long term health. Weight loss in itself does not necessarily promote health when it is accomplished by starving oneself or abstaining from consuming all of the caloric or nutritional requirements one needs in a day.

Finally, and most importantly to my mind, is that life is short and ought to be enjoyed! There is absolutely no reason why eating well has to miserable. This is the fundamental belief that underlies the whole food lifestyle. Eating simple, honest, unprocessed food whole food tastes amazing. Not only that, it is also the healthiest way to eat. Our bodies were never meant to consume the myriad multi-syllabic chemicals that populate the typical ingredient list in the processed garbage our industrial food system keep churning out. We were meant to eat real food. We were meant to eat *whole food*. This is the philosophy of the whole food lifestyle.

This book contains recipes that taste amazing, are extremely healthy, and are fully compliant with the whole food lifestyle. If you enjoy these recipes and want to learn more about the background and health benefits of the whole food lifestyle, as well as get more recipes and a complete 30 day whole food "challenge" meal plan, I recommend you consult my other book:

Whole Food: 30 Day Whole Food Challenge: AWARD WINNING Recipes for health, rapid weight loss, energy, detox, and food freedom GUARANTEED - Complete whole food diet cookbook meal plan

By Albert Pino

You can find a link to this book, and all of my books on my website:

www.albertpino.com

WHOLE FOOD BREAKFAST RECIPES

BROCCOLI TURKEY FRITTATA

Preparation time: 5 minutes
Cooking time: 25 to 30 minutes
Serves: 4 to 6

Ingredients:

- 2 cups of detached broccoli florets, blanched

- 1 cup packed baby spinach

- 8 free range organic eggs, beaten

- 1 teaspoon of extra virgin olive oil

- 1 smoked free range turkey breast fillet, precooked sliced into strips

- 1 cup of thinly sliced white onion

- 1 medium red sweet pepper, diced

- ½ teaspoon of chopped fresh thyme leaves

- ½ teaspoon of Italian seasoning

- Salt and black pepper, to taste

Directions:

1. Preheat the oven to 350°F.

2. Add the oil in an oven-safe skillet and apply medium-high heat. Sauté the onions and peppers for 2 minutes, add the turkey and season to taste with salt and pepper. Sauté for 2 minutes more and stir in the broccoli and spinach.

3. Mix the Italian seasoning and beaten eggs in a bowl and whisk until well combined. Add into the skillet and stir to combine.

4. Bake it in the oven for about 15 minutes, or until the bottom is set and the top is slightly runny.

5. Remove from the oven, cover and let it rest for 5 minutes before serving.

KALE AND BROCCOLI EGG WHITE QUICHE

Preparation time: 10 minutes

Cooking time: 40 minutes

Serves: 4

Ingredients:

- 2 cups loosely packed kale leaves

- 2 cups liquid egg whites, beaten

- 1 cup chopped broccoli

- 1 large white onion, julienned

- 1 large red sweet pepper, julienned

- 1 teaspoon garlic powder

- Salt and ground black pepper, to taste

- 2 teaspoons ghee

Directions:

1. Preheat oven to 375°F and coat a 9-inch pie dish with ghee. Set aside.

2. In a large pan, apply medium-high heat and coat the bottom with remaining ghee. Sauté the onion and pepper for 2 to 3 minutes and stir in the broccoli. Cook until the broccoli is soft and stir in the kale. Season to taste with garlic powder, salt and pepper and cook until the kale is wilted.

3. Transfer into the prepared pie dish, pour in the egg mixture and briefly stir to com-bine.

4. Bake it in the oven for about 30 minutes, or until the center is set. Remove it from the oven and let it rest for about 5 minutes before serving.

SMOKED SALMON FRITTATA WITH AVOCADO

Preparation time: 1 5 minutes
Cooking time: 10 minutes
Serves: 4

Ingredients:

- 1 tablespoon of grass fed ghee

- 6 free range eggs, beaten

- 1 large fillet of smoked salmon, flaked

- Salt and black pepper, to taste

- 1 teaspoon mixed Italian herbs

- 1 large tomato, diced

- 1 medium red onion, diced

- 1 stem of green onion, chopped

Directions:

1. In a skillet, apply medium-low heat and add the ghee. Swirl to coat the skillet evenly with ghee and sauté the onions and tomatoes until soft and tender.

2. Stir in the flaked salmon and Italian herbs, cook for 3 minutes and transfer to plate.

3. Season the egg mixture with salt and pepper and pour into the skillet. Swirl to coat evenly the bottom of the skillet add the salmon-vegetable mixture.

4. Reduce to the low heat, cover the skillet and cook until the bottom is lightly golden and the edges starts to pull away.

5. Slide unto a serving plate, cut into four wedges and top with green onions serving.

BLACKBERRY PUDDING WITH CHIA AND PISTACHIOS

Preparation time: 5 minutes

Cooking time: N/A

Serves: 2

Ingredients:

- 1 cup of almond milk
- 1 packet of unsweetened acai puree
- ½ teaspoon of vanilla extract
- ½ teaspoon cinnamon
- 1 cup of sliced fresh blackberries
- 2 tablespoons of chia seeds
- ¼ cup shredded coconut
- ¼ cup of chopped raw pistachios, for the topping

Directions:

1. Combine all ingredients in a large bowl, except for the pistachios and mix until well combined. Cover the bowl and refrigerate for at least 12 hours before serving.

2. Remove from the fridge, divide into two serving bowls and serve the blackberry pudding with chopped pistachios on top.

MANGO LASSI SMOOTHIE

Preparation time: 5 minutes

Serves: 2

Ingredients:

- 3 cups diced frozen mango
- 1 to 1 ½ cups unsweetened cashew or almond milk
- Salt and cardamom powder, to taste
- Fresh mint leaves, for serving (optional)

Directions:

1. Add the mango and cashew milk in a high-speed blender. Turn to medium-low speed and pulse for 30 seconds. Season mixture to taste with salt and cardamom, adjust to high speed and pulse until thick and smooth.

2. Transfer into two serving glasses and garnish with fresh mint on top. Serve immediately.

TANGERINE PEACH GREEN SMOOTHIE

Preparation time: 5 minutes

Serves: 2

Ingredients:

- 3 cups of sliced peach
- 1 tangerine, peeled and segmented
- 1 cup packed fresh kale
- 1 cup unsweetened almond milk
- ½ cup of fresh orange juice (optional)

Directions:

1. Add the peach, tangerine segments, kale and almond milk in a high-speed blender and pulse for 30 seconds on medium-low speed.

2. Turn to high speed and pulse until thick and smooth. Transfer into serving glasses and serve immediately.

.

BERRY SMOOTHIE AND CINNAMON TOAST

Preparation time: 5 minutes

Serves: 1-2

Ingredients:

- 1.5 cups plain organic yogurt

- 1 cup berries, fresh or frozen (blueberries, raspberries, or any other berry you life)

- 2 bananas

- 2 tablespoons milk

- 0.5 to 0.75 cup fresh spinach leaves

Directions:

1. Combine all ingredients into blender and blend until smooth.

2. Drink with a piece of cinnamon raisin toast, or other whole grain toast with cinnamon sprinkled on it. You could also spread a nut butter on the toast if you want some additional flavor.

AVOCADO COCONUT SMOOTHIE

Preparation time: 5 minutes

Serves: 2

Ingredients:

- 1 cup unsweetened coconut cream
- 2 large ripe mangoes, pitted and diced
- 1 ripe avocado, pitted and diced
- ½ teaspoon pure vanilla extract
- 1 teaspoon shredded coconut flakes, for topping

Directions:

1. Add the avocado, mango, vanilla extract, coconut cream in a high-speed blender. Turn to medium-low speed and pulse for about 30 seconds.

2. Switch to high speed and pulse until thick and smooth. Transfer into two serving glasses, top with coconut flakes and serve immediately.

MIXED BERRY SMOOTHIE

Preparation Time: 5 minutes
Serves: 2

Ingredients:

- 2 cups frozen blueberry

- 1 cup frozen raspberries

- ½ cup frozen blackberries

- 2 tablespoons dried Goji berries

- 2 tablespoon almond butter

- 1 ½ cups unsweetened cashew milk

Directions:

1. Add all ingredients in the high-speed blender or food processor. Pulse for 30 seconds on medium-low speed, turn to high and pulse until thick and smooth.

2. Transfer into two serving glasses and serve immediately.

SPINACH OMELET AND AVOCADO

Preparation Time: 10 minutes
Serves: 1

Ingredients:

- 2 eggs (best if you can purchase them from a local farmer's market)

- 2 Avocados

- Handful of organic spinach

- Big pinch of parsley

Directions:

1. Mix the yolks and egg whites in a bowl (or discard the yolks if you prefer).
2. Pour eggs into a frying pan heated to medium-low. Heat until eggs are no longer runny, at least 3 minutes.
3. Top with spinach leaves and parsley.
4. Slice both avocados in half, garnish, and serve.

BERRY BAKED CUSTARD

Preparation Time: 40 minutes

Serves: 4

Ingredients:

- 4 eggs (preferably from a local farmer's market)

- 1 cup of Greek yogurt

- 0.5 teaspoons of vanilla powder

- Finely grated zest of one lemon

- 30 blueberries, fresh or frozen (thawed overnight in the fridge)

Directions:

1. Preheat your oven to 390 F.

2. In a food processor or blender, mix the eggs, yogurt, vanilla and lemon zest for 45 seconds.

3. Grease the ramekins with a small amount of almond butter.

4. Pour the mixture into four ramekins. Place the ramekins in a large ovenproof pan with lid, filled with water such that the water level reaches the top quarter of the ramekins.

5. Place some fruit in each ramekin.

6. Cover with the lid and bake for about 30 minutes or until the middle is set and beginning to rise.

BANANA APPLE GREEN SMOOTHIE

Preparation time: 5 minutes
Serves: 2

Ingredients:

- 2 large ripe banana, peeled and sliced
- 2 large green apples, cored and sliced
- 1 cup almond milk
- 1 cup packed fresh kale
- ¼ teaspoon of cinnamon

Directions:

1. Add all ingredients in a high-speed blender or food processor and pulse for 30 seconds on medium-low speed.

2. Adjust to high speed and pulse until thick and smooth. Transfer into two serving glasses and sprinkle with cinnamon on top. Serve immediately.

TACO-SPICED TURKEY BURRITO

Preparation time: 10 minutes
Cooking time: 15 minutes
Serves: 4

Ingredients:

- 1 pound free range ground turkey
- 1 tablespoon of taco seasoning
- 1 teaspoon poultry seasoning
- Salt and black pepper, to taste
- 1 tablespoons grass fed ghee
- 4 gluten-free flour tortillas
- 1 red sweet pepper, minced
- 1 medium white onion, minced
- 1 stem green onions, chopped
- 2 tablespoons of salsa
- 1 ripe tomato, sliced
- 1 ripe avocado, sliced

Directions:

1. Add the ground turkey, taco and poultry seasoning in a bowl. Season to taste with salt and pepper and mix until well combined.

2. Add the ghee in a medium skillet and apply medium-high heat. Cook the ground turkey until lightly brown and cooked through. Remove from skillet and add the sweet pepper, white onion and green onions in the same skillet, sauté for about 5 minutes. Remove from pan, transfer to the bowl with the ground turkey and mix until well combined.

3. In the same pan, heat the tortillas for 1 minute on each side and place it on a flat work surface.

4. Divide the meat mixture, salsa, tomato and avocado on each tortilla and roll up to form into burritos. Slice into halves, transfer to a serving plate and serve immediately.

ALMOND RAISIN OATMEAL

Preparation time: 5 minutes

Serves: 1

Ingredients:

- Steel cut oatmeal

- Handful of raisins

- Handful of almonds

- Cinnamon

Directions:

1. Prepare the oatmeal according to the instructions on the package.

2. When the oatmeal is halfway finished cooking, add the raisins and almonds.

3. When finished cooking, add cinnamon to taste

BAKED APPLE PANCAKES

Preparation time: 10 minutes

Cooking time: 20 minutes

Serves: 2

Ingredients:

- 2 Granny Smith apples, peeled and sliced paper thin
- Approximately 4 tablespoons of almond butter, enough to cover your pan
- 3 eggs (preferably from a local farmer's market)
- 1 cup of coconut milk
- 2 teaspoons of cinnamon
- 1 teaspoon of juice from freshly squeezed lemon
- 1 teaspoon of vanilla powder
- half a teaspoon of sea salt
- half a teaspoon of bicarbonate of soda
- 2 cups of almond meal

Directions:

1. Preheat oven to 350 F.
2. In an oven-proof pan melt the almond butter. It should coat the base of the pan completely.
3. Cover the base of the pan in a single layer of apple slices. Sprinkle cinnamon over the apple slices.

4. In a blender or food processor, combine the eggs, milk, almond meal, remaining sugar, cinnamon, vanilla, sea salt, bicarbonate of soda. vinegar and mix until thoroughly combined.

5. Pour the mix over the apple slices.

6. Bake in your preheated oven for approximately 20 minutes or until the middle of the pancake is set.

MUSHROOM AND SPINACH FRITTATA

Preparation time: 10 minutes
Cooking time: 20 minutes
Serves: 4

Ingredients:

- 1 tablespoon ghee
- ½ cup of sliced button mushrooms
- ¼ cup minced shallot
- 2 cups loosely packed baby spinach
- 6 free range organic eggs
- ¼ almond milk
- Salt and pepper, to taste
- ½ teaspoon mixed Italian herbs
- 1 tomato, sliced into rounds
- 1 cup of precooked free range chicken breast, diced

Directions:

1. Add the ghee in a skillet and apply medium-high heat. Sauté the shallot, mushroom and spinach for 5 minutes.

2. While sautéing the vegetables, whisk the eggs, milk, Italian herbs, a pinch of salt and pepper in a bowl and pour it into the skillet. Top with diced chicken and tomatoes, cover skillet and reduce heat to low.

3. Cook for about 10 minutes, or until the eggs are set and the bottom is lightly brown. Remove the skillet from heat and let it stand for 5 minutes with cover.

4. Slide the frittata on a serving plate, slice into 4 wedges and serve warm.

TASTY AND HEALTHY WHOLE WHEAT BREAKFAST CREPES

Preparation time: 15 minutes

Serves: 2-4

Ingredients:

- 3 eggs (preferably from a local farmer's market)
- 1 cup whole-wheat flour
- 1 cup almond milk
- 1 teaspoon vanilla
- A quarter of a teaspoon of salt
- Half a cup of water
- 2 tablespoons of melted almond butter

Directions:

1. Put all of the ingredients in your blender and mix them thoroughly. Let the mix stand for 10 minutes.

2. Coat your frying pan with almond butter over medium heat.

3. Pour the batter on your pan held at an angle. Swirl the batter around to coat the entire the pan in one thin layer.

4. Push down the thin edges of the crepe around the perimeter using a spatula.

5. After 45 seconds to 1 minute when the crepe is golden brown on the bottom, flip it over. Do this delicately to avoid ripping the crepe.

6. Cook another 45 seconds on the other side and then roll up each crepe.

MEATBALLS IN TOMATO BASIL SAUCE

Preparation time: 15 minutes
Cooking time: 15 minutes
Serves: 4

Ingredients:

- 2 cups tomato basil sauce
- ¼ cup fresh basil leaves, chopped
- ½ cup grass fed beef bone broth
- 1 tablespoon olive oil

For the Meatballs:

- 1 pound grass fed ground beef
- 1 large free range egg
- 1 small onion, minced
- 1 teaspoon minced garlic
- Salt and black pepper, to taste
- ½ teaspoon mixed Italian herbs
- 1 tablespoon Italian meatball seasoning

Directions:

1. Mix all meatball ingredients in a large bowl and chill for at least 2 hours before cooking. Divide into 8 portions and form into large balls.

2. Add the oil in a skillet and apply medium-high heat. Cook the meatballs for about 6 to 8 minutes while turning regularly until lightly browned and cooked through. Transfer to a plate and set aside.

3. Add the tomato sauce, broth and basil in the same skillet and cook until reaches to a boil. Add the meatballs, reduce to low heat and simmer for about 8 to 10 minutes.

4. Transfer to a serving platter and serve immediately.

RASPBERRY CHIA SEED PUDDING

Preparation time: 5 minutes

Serves: 1

Ingredients:

- 1.5 cups fresh or frozen raspberries (if frozen, thaw overnight in the fridge)
- 1.5 cups of coconut milk
- 0.5 cups of chia seeds
- 1 teaspoon of vanilla powder
- 0.25 cups of brown rice syrup (according to taste)

Directions:

1. Mix all ingredients thoroughly in a blender.
2. Refrigerate overnight to allow the mix to thicken.
3. Consume in the morning for a fast, simple, delicious, and healthy breakfast!

.

MEXICAN BENEDICT CHIPOTLE SAUCE

Preparation time: 10 minutes
Cooking time: 5 minutes
Serves: 4

Ingredients:

- 2 chipotle peppers, seeded and diced
- 3 free range organic egg yolks
- ½ tablespoon of lime juice
- ½ cup of ghee
- 4 poached free range eggs
- 1 tablespoon of olive oil
- 4 cups loosely packed baby spinach
- Salt and ground black pepper, to taste

For Serving:

- 1 avocado, sliced
- 2 tablespoons minced fresh cilantro

Directions:

1. Add the chipotle, egg yolks and lime juice in a blender and blend until smooth and well incorporated. Pulse again while gradually adding the ghee until a thick and smooth consistency is achieved.

2. In a skillet, apply medium-high heat and add the oil. Add the spinach and cook for 3 minutes or until wilted. Season to taste with salt and pepper.

3. Portion the spinach into 4 serving plates, top with poached egg and drizzle with sauce on top.

4. Serve warm with avocado slices and cilantro.

CREAMY CASHEW PARFAIT

Preparation time: 5 minutes

Serves: 1

Ingredients:

- 1 cup of muesli

- 1 cup of cashew nut cream

- 1 cup of mixed frozen berries (do not thaw)

- Quarter of a cup of toasted almond flakes

- Ground cinnamon (to taste)

Directions:

1. Simply combine the ingredients, stir, and serve!

EGG WHITE OMELETTE WITH SHREDDED CHICKEN AND APPLE

Preparation time: 10 minutes

Cooking time: 15 minutes

Serves: 2

Ingredients:

- 1 teaspoon of ghee
- 1 cup of free range egg whites, beaten
- 1 cup of precooked free range chicken breast
- 1 green apple, cored and peeled, diced
- 1 cup shredded collard greens
- ¼ cup of toasted almonds, chopped
- Salt and black pepper, to taste

Directions:

1. In a pan, apply medium-high heat and add the ghee. Add the chicken, season with salt and pepper and cook until the meat is golden brown. Stir in the apples and cook for 1 minute or until soft and tender. Transfer to a plate and set aside.

2. Add the collard greens in the pan, cook for 2 minutes and return the chicken and apple.

3. Pour the egg whites in the skillet, swirl to spread evenly on the bottom of the pan and top with crushed hazelnuts.

4. Cover and reduce to low heat. Cook for about 5 minutes or until the eggs are set and cooked through.

5. Slide it on a serving plate and serve the omelette immediately.

OAT CRANBERRY SMOOTHIE

Preparation time: 5
Serves: 1

Ingredients:

- 1 quarter cup of cranberries (fresh or frozen)
- 2 tablespoons rolled oats
- 1 cup almond milk
- Half a pear
- Dash of cinnamon (to taste)

Directions:

1. Simply combine all of the ingredients in a blender and blend until smooth. Enjoy!

BREAKFAST TURKEY CASSEROLE

Preparation time: 20 minutes
Cooking time: 40 minutes
Serves: 4 to 6

Ingredients:

- 6 large free range eggs

- 1 large red tomato, diced

- 1 white onion, thinly sliced

- 1 teaspoon of garlic powder

- 1 cup diced green sweet pepper

- 1 cup diced red sweet pepper

- ½ cup coconut milk

For the Meat:

- 1 pound free range ground turkey meat

- 1 teaspoon poultry seasoning

- 1 tablespoon of meatloaf seasoning

- Salt and ground black pepper, to taste

Directions:

1. Preheat oven to 350°F.

2. Add all ingredients for the meat in a bowl, season to taste with salt and pepper and mix thoroughly until well combined.

3. In a pan over medium-high heat, cook the meat mixture for 6 minutes while stirring regularly until lightly browned. Remove with a slotted spoon and transfer to a plate, leaving the oil and set aside.

4. In the same pan, sauté the onions, tomato and peppers until for 5 minutes and return the meat mixture. Remove from heat, transfer to greased baking dish and spread evenly on the bottom.

5. In a large bowl, whisk the eggs, milk, garlic powder and season to taste with salt and pepper. Pour egg mixture over the ground meat and spread evenly on top. Bake it in the oven for 40 to 45 minutes, or until the dish is thoroughly cooked.

6. Remove from the oven, transfer to a wire rack and let it rest for 5 minutes before serving.

GROUND BEEF CASSEROLE WITH CASHEWS

Preparation time: 10 minutes
Cooking time: 45 to 45 minutes
Serves: 4

Ingredients:

- 1 pound of grass fed beef, ground

- ½ cup chopped cashews

- 1 cup homemade grass fed beef stock or broth

- 1 cup canned cream of mushroom

- 2 tablespoons of olive oil

- 2 tablespoons meatloaf seasoning mix

Directions:

1. Preheat the oven to 325 °F and grease a 9x23 inch casserole with 1 tablespoon of oil.

2. In a pan, apply medium-high heat and add 1 tablespoon of oil with the ground beef. Cook for about 6 to 7 minutes while stirring occasionally until lightly browned.

3. Add 1 ½ tablespoons of meatloaf seasoning and cook for 2 minutes while stirring regularly. Pour in the mushroom, stock and cream of mushrooms.

4. Cover the pan, adjust seasoning by adding slowly the spice mix until the desired taste is achieved and bring it to a boil.

5. Transfer into a greased 9x13 inch casserole and briefly stir just to combine. Top with cashews, bake it in the oven for about 30 minutes or until thoroughly cooked.

6. Remove from the oven and let it stand for 10 minutes before serving.

BANANA QUINOA

Preparation time: 10 minutes
Serves: 1

Ingredients:

- 1 cup cooked quinoa

- 1 cup almond milk

- Handful of raisins

- Dash of cinnamon (to taste)

Directions:

1. Use a small pan or pot and bring quinoa, milk, raisins, and cinnamon to a gentle boil.
2. Once boiling, reduce the heat and simmer, stirring the mix frequently for about five minutes.
3. You'll know it is done when about half the milk has been absorbed. Garnish with fresh slices of banana and serve.

GRILLED CHICKEN PATTIES

Preparation time: 10 minutes

Cooking time: 15 minutes

Serves: 4

Ingredients:

- 1 pound free range chicken meat, ground

- 1 free range egg

- 1 tablespoon of mixed Italian herbs

- ¼ cup gluten free breadcrumbs

- Salt and ground black pepper, to taste

- 1 teaspoon poultry seasoning

- Olive oil, for greasing

Directions:

1. Combine together all spices in a large bowl and mix thoroughly until well combined. Add the ground meat and mix until all ingredients are well incorporated. Taste and adjust the seasonings if needed and chill for at least 2 hours.

2. Divide the meat mixture into 4 portions and roll them into balls. Lightly press down to form into patties and set aside.

3. Preheat the gas grill to high, lightly brush the grill with oil and reduce to medium heat. Grill the patties for 5 to 6

minutes on each side and flip to cook the other side for 5 minutes more.

4. Remove the patties from the grill, transfer to a plate and let it rest for 5 minutes. Serve with whole wheat burger or brioche bun, if desired.

TURKEY BREAST AVOCADO SANDWICH

Preparation time: 15 minutes
Cooking time: 15 minutes
Serves: 4

Ingredients:

- 1 free range organic turkey breast half, thinly sliced
- Salt and pepper, to taste
- 1 teaspoon of poultry seasoning
- 1 tablespoon of ghee
- 8 slices of gluten-free sandwich bread
- 2 tablespoons of green chili sauce

Toppings:

- Avocado slices
- Tomato slices
- Lettuce leaves

DIRECTIONS:

1. Rub the meat with salt, pepper and poultry seasoning on both sides. Add the ghee in a skillet over medium-high heat and fry the turkey breast for 4 minutes on each side. Remove from skillet and let it rest for 10 minutes before slicing.

2. Spread the chili sauce on one side of four slices of bread, place the pan-fried turkey and add the toppings.

3. Cut the sandwich across the diagonal, transfer to a serving platter and serve immediately.

BLUEBERRY-BANANA ACAI BOWL

Preparation Time: 10 minutes
Cooking Time: N/A
Serves: 4

Ingredients:

For the Acai Mixture:

- 1 pack of unsweetened frozen acai puree, thawed

- 2 cup fresh blueberries

- 2 ripe bananas

- 2 cups of vanilla almond milk

For the Toppings:

- 1 tablespoon of teaspoon cacao nibs

- 2 tablespoons of chopped almonds

Directions:

1. Place all ingredients for the acai mixture in a high speed blender or food processor, and pulse until thick and smooth. Transfer to a bowl, cover and chill for at least 2 hours.

2. Divide into four serving bowls, topping almonds and cacao nibs and serve immediately.

SAUTÉED ASPARAGUS AND FRIED HEMP FU

Preparation Time: 10 minutes
Cooking Time: 15 minutes
Serves: 4

Ingredients:

- 1 pound of fresh asparagus spears
- 12 ounces Hemp Tofu, cut into ½-inch slices
- 1 tablespoon of olive oil,
- 1 teaspoon minced garlic
- 1 red onion, diced
- ¼ cup grass fed beef stock or broth
- 1 tablespoon balsamic vinegar
- 2 tablespoon raw coconut aminos
- Salt and pepper, to taste
- 1 tablespoon of lime juice
- 2 tablespoons of pine nuts

Directions:

1. Add ½ tablespoon of oil in skillet over medium-high heat. Season the hemp tofu with salt and pepper and pan-fry for

4 minutes on each side. Turn to cook the other side and transfer to a plate.

2. Add the remaining oil in the same skillet and sauté the onion and garlic for 2 minutes. Add the asparagus, coconut aminos, stock and vinegar and cook for 5 minutes while turning regularly, until the asparagus are tender and the liquid has reduced in half.

3. Return the hemp tofu and add the pine nuts. Cook for about 2 minutes and remove from heat.

4.   Divide into four serving plates, drizzle with lime juice and serve warm.

WHOLE FOOD LUNCH RECIPES

CITRUS PEPPERED SHRIMPS

Preparation time: 5 minutes
Cooking time: 10 minutes
Serves: 4

Ingredients:

- 1 pound wild-caught shrimps, peeled and deveined
- 1 tablespoon of olive oil
- 2 tablespoons minced parsley, for serving
- 4 wedges of lemons, for serving

For the Marinade:

- 1 large lemon, juiced and zested
- 1 teaspoon black peppercorns, crushed
- ½ teaspoon salt
- 1 teaspoon smoked paprika
- 1 teaspoon crushed red pepper flakes

Directions:

1. Combine all marinade ingredients in a large bowl and add in the shrimps. Toss to evenly coat the shrimps with marinade and chill for at least 1 to 2 hours before cooking.

2. In a large wok over high heat, add the oil when the wok is very hot. Stir fry the shrimps for about 5 minutes, or until the flesh is opaque and thoroughly cooked.

3. Transfer into a serving platter, garnish with minced parsley and serve with lemon wedges.

SALMON WITH CURRIED TOMATOES

Preparation time: 5 minutes
Cooking time: 20 minutes
Serves: 4

Ingredients:

- 2 tablespoons grass fed ghee or olive oil

- 4 large fresh wild Atlantic salmon fillets

- ½ cup loosely packed fresh basil, cut into chiffonade

- 3 tablespoons Thai red curry paste

- 1 cup halved grape tomatoes

- 1 teaspoon mixed Italian herbs

- Salt and black pepper, to taste

Directions:

1. Preheat the oven to a temperature of 400°F. Lightly grease a rimmed baking sheet with oil and set aside.

2. Lightly brush both sides of the fillets with oil, then with 2 tablespoons of curry paste and season to taste with salt and pepper.

3. Add the tomatoes, Italian herbs, 1 tablespoon of oil and curry paste and season to taste with salt and pepper. Spread evenly on the greased baking tray. Place the fillet on top of the tomatoes and cook it in the oven for 20 minutes.

4. It is done when the fish flakes easily with a fork. Divide the tomatoes on four serving plates, place one fillet on top and serve with fresh basil leaves over each fillet.

KALE AND TOMATO STUFFED CHICKEN BREASTS

Preparation time: 5 minutes
Cooking time: 30 minutes
Serves: 4

Ingredients:

- 2 whole free range organic chicken breasts (skinless and boneless), halved

- Salt and black pepper, to taste

- 1 teaspoon poultry seasoning

- 2 tablespoons of ghee or olive oil

- ½ cup of fresh kale, minced

- ¼ cup chopped sun-dried tomatoes

- ¼ cup of cashew butter

- ¼ cup of salsa sauce

Directions:

1. Preheat an oven to a temperature of 400°F. Lightly grease a rimmed baking tray with oil and set aside.

2. Add ½ cup of water into a pan, apply medium-high heat and bring to a boil. Add the kale, dried tomatoes and ½ tablespoon of oil and cook until the kale is wilted and the tomatoes have softened. Season to taste with salt and pepper and remove the pan from heat.

3. Flattened the halved chicken breast with a meat mallet and season both sides with salt, pepper and poultry seasoning. Divide the kale-tomato mixture and cashew butter on four chicken breasts, roll it up and secure the end with toothpick.

4. Lightly brush the outer part with oil and transfer into the greased baking tray. Bake for about 25 minutes or until lightly golden and cooked through.

5. Remove from the oven, let it rest for 5 minutes and cut into halves or thin slices.

6. Transfer to a serving plate and serve warm with tomato salsa.

SHREDDED YELLOW CURRY CHICKEN SALAD

Preparation time: 5 minutes

Serves: 1-2

Ingredients:

- 3 cups chicken, cooked and shredded

- ½ cup plain yogurt

- 1 teaspoon yellow curry powder

- Handful of cilantro leaves, thoroughly washed

- Handful of sliced almonds

Directions:

1. Simply combine the ingredients and toss for a delicious salad.

2. If you'd like to add dressing, you can make your own simple, tasty, healthy dressing by combining 1 tablespoon of extra virgin olive oil mixed with 2 teaspoons of balsamic vinegar.

TURKEY LETTUCE WRAPS

Preparation time: 5 minutes
Cooking time: 25 minutes
Serves: 4 to 6

Ingredients:

- 1 pound free range ground lean turkey

- 1 teaspoon mixed Italian herbs

- 1 tablespoon taco seasoning

- 1 large red onion, minced

- 1 small red sweet pepper, minced

- 1 cup of tomato concasse

- 4 to 6 Crisphead lettuce leaves

- 1 teaspoon of oil, for greasing

- ½ cup of free range chicken bone broth or stock

Directions:

1. In a non-stick pan over medium-high heat, add the ground turkey and cook until lightly browned and the pan juices have reduced. Stir in the Italian herbs, taco seasoning onions, sweet pepper and tomato and cook it for 5 minutes while stirring regularly.

2. Pour in the broth or stock, cover with lid and bring it to a boil. Reduce the heat to low and simmer for about 20

minutes, or until the liquid has reduced in half. Remove the pan from heat and set it aside.

3. Prepare the lettuce leaves and place them on a work surface. Portion the meat into the 6 to 8 lettuce leaves, and then place it in the center.

4. Serve the lettuce wraps with avocado, tomato salsa or according to preference.

SMASHED GARLIC PINTO BEAN PITA

Preparation time: 10 minutes
Cooking time: 8 hours
Serves: 1 to 2

Ingredients:

- 1 onion, chopped

- 2 cups dry pinto beans (make sure you rinse them well and check for rocks)

- Handful of fresh jalapeno peppers, chopped

- 4 cloves garlic, smashed and minced

- 1 teaspoon black pepper

- 1 teaspoon chili pepper

- 2 tablespoons of cumin

- 6 cups of water or your favorite broth

Directions:

1. Combine all ingredients in slow cooker and cook on high for at least 6 hours (8 hours is best).

2. Drain any excess liquid. Serve in a bowl or in a warm, whole wheat pita.

ONION-MUSHROOMS BEEF TIPS

Preparation time: 10 minutes
Cooking time: 30 to 40 minutes
Serves: 4

Ingredients:

- 1 pound grass-fed lean beef stew, cut into large cubes

- 2 tablespoons of olive oil

- Salt and black pepper, to taste

- 2 cups of fresh shiitake mushrooms

- 2 cups of grass fed beef bone broth or stock

- 1 medium white onion, sliced into rings

- 1 tablespoon minced garlic

Directions:

1. Season the beef with salt and pepper and toss to coat it evenly with spices.

2. In a stew pot over medium-high heat, add the oil and brown the beef evenly on all sides. Stir in the garlic and onions, sauté for 2 minutes and add the mushrooms

3. Add the oil in the inner pot, press the sauté button and adjust to brown mode. Season beef with salt and pepper and brown evenly on all sides in the inner pot. Stir in the onions and garlic and sauté for about 1 minute and then add the mushrooms and the stock. Cover with lid, bring it to a

boil and reduce to low heat. Simmer for about 30 minutes or until the meat is tender and cooked through.

4. Adjust the seasoning and transfer into a serving bowl. Serve immediately.

LIVELY PUMPKIN SEED SALAD

Preparation time: 10 minutes

Serves: 1

Ingredients:

- 3 cups of your favorite lettuce leaves, mixed greens, or spinach

- 0.25 cups roasted pumpkin seeds

- 0.25 cups currants

- Dressing: 1 tablespoon extra virgin olive oil mixed with 2 teaspoons balsamic vinegar

Directions:

1. Simply chop the lettuce, mix all ingredients and serve!

SALMON, AVOCADO AND CUCUMBER GREEN SALAD

Preparation time: 10 minutes
Cooking time: 10 minutes
Serves: 2

Ingredients:

- 1 fillet wild Atlantic salmon, skinless
- ¼ teaspoon garlic powder
- ¼ teaspoon Italian seasoning
- Salt and black pepper, to taste
- 1 lime, juiced
- 2 teaspoons grass fed ghee
- 2 cups loosely packed ~~fresh kale, cut into chiffonade~~ baby spring lettuce
- 1 ripe avocado, cubed add tomatoes
- 1 small cucumber, sliced into rounds
- 2 tablespoons minced parsley

For the Dressing:

- 2 tablespoons of olive oil
- 1 lime, juiced
- Salt and pepper
- ~~1 tablespoon~~ minced dill
  ½ teaspoon
- balsamic vinegar

Directions:

1. Season the salmon with salt, pepper, garlic powder and Italian seasoning and drizzle with lime juice on both sides.

2. Add the ghee in a skillet over medium-high heat and fry the salmon for about 3 minutes on each side. Remove from skillet, let it rest for 5 minutes on a plate and cut into cubes.

3. Whisk all dressing ingredients in a large bowl, add in the rest of the ingredients and gently toss to evenly coat the salad ingredients with dressing.

4. Divide into four serving bowls, top with salmon and serve immediately.

VEAL SCALLOPS AND ZUCCHINI ROLL UPS

Preparation time: 15 minutes
Cooking time: 15 minutes
Serves: 4

Ingredients:

- 8 slices of veal scallops
- 1 zucchini, halved crosswise and quartered
- 1 teaspoon olive oil
- Salt and black pepper

For the Marinade:

- 1 teaspoon pepper steak grill seasoning
- 1 tablespoon lime juice
- 1 tablespoon nama shoyu
- 2 tablespoons balsamic vinegar
- 2 tablespoons of olive oil

Directions:

1. Flatten the veal scallops using a meat mallet and season both sides with salt and pepper.

2. Add all marinade ingredients in a bowl and whisk until well combined. Add the veal, coat evenly with marinade mixture and let it stand for 1 to 2 hours.

3. Preheat grill to high heat and lightly brush the grill with oil.

4. Lightly brush the zucchini with oil and season to taste with salt and pepper. Grill for 3 minutes while turning regularly, remove from grill and let it rest to cool on a plate.

5. Tightly wrap the zucchini with veal scallop and secure the end with a toothpick. Grill veal rolls for 6 while turning regularly until the meat is thoroughly cooked.

6. Remove from grill, transfer to a serving platter and discard the toothpick. Cut into halves and serve immediately.

PERFECT PESTO PASTA

Preparation time: 5 minutes
Cooking time: 15 minutes
Serves: 2

Ingredients:

- Two cups of fresh sweet peas, cooked
- 1/2 cup extra virgin olive oil
- 1 handful of fresh basil
- 3 cloves of garlic, minced
- Quarter cup pine nuts
- Half teaspoon tsp onion powder
- Half teaspoon garlic powder
- Quarter cup red onion, finely diced
- Handful of fresh cherry tomatoes
- Pinch of sea salt
- Your favorite pasta

Directions:

1. Mix the cooked sweet peas, basil, pine nuts, olive oil, garlic, onion powder and garlic powder in your blender.

2. Heat one tablespoon of extra virgin olive oil in a pan over medium heat. Add diced onion to the pan.

3. After cooking for five minutes, add the cooked onion to the blender and blend.

4. Cook your pasta, then simply add your pesto from the blender to the cooked pasta, garnish with cherry tomatoes, toss thoroughly, and serve.

PEPPERED LEMON-LIME CHICKEN BREAST

Preparation time: 15 minutes
Cooking time: 15 minutes
Serves: 4

Ingredients:

- 2 free range chicken breasts (skinless and boneless), halved

For the Marinade:

- 2 tablespoons of olive oil
- 1 lemon, juiced
- 1 lime, juiced
- 1 teaspoon poultry seasoning
- 2 teaspoons of minced garlic
- 1 medium onion, minced
- 1 teaspoon black peppercorns, crushed

Directions:

1. Add all marinade ingredients in mixing bowl and whisk until well combined. Add chicken, coat evenly with marinade and let it stand for about 1 to 2 hours.

2. Preheat grill to high and lightly brush the grill with oil.

3. Reduce to medium heat and grill the chicken for about 6 to 8 minutes on each side. Turn to cook the other side and occasionally brush with marinade mixture while grilling.

4. When the chicken is done, transfer to a plate and let it rest for 5 minutes with a tent foil.

5. Slice and transfer to a plate and serve immediately.

KALE WRAPPED NAVY BEANS

Preparation time: 5 minutes
Cooking time: 30 minutes
Serves: 2

Ingredients:

- 3 tbsp extra virgin olive oil

- 1 cup chopped onions

- 5 Cloves of garlic, minced

- 2-3 fresh whole tomatoes, blended

- 4 fresh basil leaves, chopped

- Half teaspoon ground sage

- 2 cups cooked navy beans (cook for 6-8 hours in slow cooker)

Directions:

1. Add 3 tablespoons of olive oil and chopped onions to pot with lid and warm over low heat

2. Add garlic and saute until fragrant but not burnt.

3. Add tomatoes, sage, and basil leaves, stir and simmer for 5 minutes.

4. Add cooked beans

5. Stir and simmer for 20 minutes

6. Spoon mix into leaves of kale, wrap and serve

SKIRT STEAK WITH CHIMICHURRI SAUCE

Preparation time: 10 minutes
Cooking time: 15 minutes
Serves: 2

Ingredients:

For the Steak:

- 1 pound grass fed beef flank steak, trimmed
- Salt and crushed black pepper

For the Sauce:

- ½ cup minced fresh parsley
- ½ cup minced fresh cilantro
- ½ cup of extra virgin olive oil
- 3 tablespoons of apple cider vinegar
- 2 teaspoons of minced garlic
- 1 teaspoon of crushed red pepper flakes
- ½ teaspoon of salt
- ½ teaspoon of crushed black pepper

Directions:

1. Add all sauce ingredients in a food processor and pulse until a coarse mixture is achieved. Transfer into a bowl and set aside.

2. Preheat grill to high and lightly brush the grid with oil.

3. Season the steak evenly with salt and crushed black pepper and grill for 5 to 6 minutes on each side. Turn and grill the other side for 5 to 6 minutes.

4. Check for safe internal temperature before removing from the grill. Cook until it reaches 270°F/135°C for medium rare.

5. When the steak is done, transfer to a cutting board and let it rest for 5 minutes.

6. Thinly slice the steak across the grain and transfer into a serving platter. Serve the grilled steak with Chimichurri sauce.

JERKED LAMB RIB CHOPS

Preparation time: 10 minutes
Cooking time: 20 minutes
Serves: 4

Ingredients:

- 4 grass fed lamb rib/loin chops
- Fleur de sel and black pepper, to taste

For the Marinade:

- 1 tablespoon minced garlic
- ¼ cup minced onion
- 1 tablespoon minced fresh rosemary
- 2 Scotch bonnet peppers, seeded and minced
- 1 stem spring onion, coarsely chopped
- 1 teaspoon of ground allspice
- 2 tablespoons ghee

Directions:

1. Season the both sides of the lamb with fleur de sel and pepper.

2. Add all marinade ingredients in a food processor and pulse until the ingredients are coarsely ground well combined. Transfer into a bowl, add the lamb and coat evenly with marinade mixture. Cover and let it stand for an hour.

3. Preheat the grill to high heat and brush the grill with oil. Grill the lamb chops for 8 to 10 minutes on each side and turn to cook the other side for 8 minutes, or until done.

4. Remove from grill, transfer to a plate and let it rest for 5 minutes before serving.

RED LENTIL SOUP

Preparation time: 5 minutes

Cooking time: 5 hours

Serves: 2

Ingredients:

- 1 cup red lentils, washed thoroughly
- 3 celery stalks, chopped
- 1 large onion, chopped
- 2 large carrots, chopped
- 2 tablespoons of tomato paste
- 2 cups of broccoli florets
- Pinch of oregano
- 1 bay leaf
- 6 leaves of basil, chopped
- Pinch of ground thyme
- 5 cups water

Directions:

1. Simply combine ingredients in a slow cooker and cook for 4-5 hours on high.

GRILLED PORK CHOPS AND SWEET POTATOES

Preparation time:15 minutes
Cooking time: 20 minutes
Serves: 4

Ingredients:

For the Sweet Potato:

- 2 medium sweet potatoes, quartered

- 1 tablespoon of extra virgin olive oil

- ½ teaspoon of smoked paprika

- ½ teaspoon of ground cinnamon

- A pinch of salt

- A pinch of crushed black pepper

For the Pork Chop:

- 4 bone-in organic pasture raised pork chops

- ½ tablespoon of smoked paprika

- Salt and crushed black pepper

For the Mango Sauce:

- ½ cup pureed ripe mango

- 1 tablespoon of ghee

- 1 tablespoon of apple cider vinegar

A gift for you

Happy Birthday Emily!!! Love YOU!
Dean & Reid

amazon Gift Receipt

 ## Send a Thank You Note

You can learn more about your gift
or start a return here too.

Scan using the Amazon app or visit
http://a.co/4xsO5zE

Whole: 100 Whole Food Recipes for Health and Weight Loss
Order ID: 108-8368019-0558615   Ordered on August 25, 2016

- A pinch of ground black pepper

Directions:

1. Add all sauce ingredients in a saucepan and apply medium heat. Cook for 5 minutes or until it reaches to a boil while stirring occasionally. Transfer to a bowl and set aside.

2. In a separate bowl, add the potatoes and sprinkle with dry ingredients. Add the oil and gently toss to distribute the seasonings.

3. Season pork chops with paprika, salt and pepper on both sides and set aside.

4. Preheat gas grill to medium-high heat and brush the grill with oil.

5. Grill potatoes on one side of the grill and the pork chops on the other side. Take ½ of the mango sauce and brush both sides of the meat while grilling.

6. Grill the potatoes for 10 minutes on each side and turn to cook the other side for 10 minutes. Grill the pork chops for 6 to 8 minutes on each side, turn to cook the other side for another 6 minutes or until cooked through.

7. Place the pork chops and potatoes on a serving platter and serve with the reserved mango sauce.

DELICIOUS CAULIFLOWER AND CELERY FAT LOSS SOUP

Preparation time: 10 minutes
Cooking time: 30 minutes
Serves: 2

Ingredients:

- 1 large cauliflower (between 2 and 3 pounds)
- 3 medium onions, chopped
- 3 celery stalks, chopped
- 1 teaspoon of paprika
- 1 teaspoon of onion powder
- 1 teaspoon of garlic powder
- 2 tablespoons of coconut oil
- 1 tablespoon of white wine vinegar
- 5 cups of water
- 1 bay leaf
- 2 garlic cloves, minced
- 1 tablespoon of freshly squeezed lime juice
- Ground course sea salt according to taste

Directions:

1. Heat a medium sized dutch oven and pour in the coconut oil, then add onions and celery and cook for 3 minutes, then add garlic and cook for an additional one minute.

2. Add the vinegar and stir until it evaporates.

3. Stir in all the spices

4. Add the chopped cauliflower, salt, bay leaf, and water. Heat until it boils

5. Lower heat, cover, and simmer.

6. When the cauliflower is soft, remove bay leaf and stir to make the soup's texture more creamy, then serve

Baked Italian Chicken Fingers

Preparation time: 10 minutes

Cooking time: 20 minutes

Serves: 4 to 6

Ingredients:

- 1 ½ pounds of free range chicken tenders

- Olive or coconut oil, as needed for frying

- 2 free range eggs, beaten

For the Breading:

- 1 cup gluten-free breadcrumbs

- 1 teaspoon of garlic powder

- ¼ teaspoon black pepper

- ½ teaspoon seasoned salt

- ½ teaspoon of cayenne

- 1 teaspoon of mixed Italian herbs

Directions:

1. Preheat the oven to 380°F and line a baking sheet with parchment paper.

2. Add all breading ingredients in a bowl and beat the eggs in a separate bowl.

3. Dip the chicken in the beaten egg and dredge to coat evenly with breadcrumb mixture. Transfer to a lined a baking sheet and repeat procedure with remaining ingredients.

4. Bake it in the oven for 15 to 20 minute, or until crisp and lightly golden.

QUINOA PROTEIN POWER PATTY

Preparation time: 10 minutes
Cooking time: 10 minutes
Serves: 2 to 4

Ingredients:

- 1 cup quinoa, (make sure you wash thoroughly first!)

- 1 bunch of spring onions (dice the white portion)

- 1 cup of chopped kale

- 4 eggs, preferably from your local farmer's market

- 2 cloves of garlic, chopped

- 1 cup of your favorite fresh whole grain bread crumbs

- Ground course sea salt, to taste

- Ground pepper, to taste

Directions:

1. Cook your washed quinoa according to the instructions on the package. After it is cooked, let it cool.

2. Stir your eggs in a bowl.

3. Mix all the ingredients together, including eggs and quinoa, stirring thoroughly.

4. Heat a large frying pan over medium heat. Add some minimally processed oil such as coconut oil if you like.

5. Spoon a portion of the mixture into the pan, using a spatula to press it down into the shape of a patty.

6. Cook until the edges start to brown, then flip and cook the other side until the edges start to brown.

7. Serve alone or on a whole grain bun or pita

GRILLED T-BONES STEAKS

Preparation time: 5 minutes
Cooking time: 15 minutes
Serves: 4

Ingredients:

- 4 grass fed beef T-bone steaks

- Ghee, for greasing

For the Dry Rub:

- 2 tablespoons of smoked paprika

- 1 teaspoon of onion powder

- 1 teaspoon of garlic powder

- 1 teaspoon of chili powder

- 1 teaspoon of ground coriander

- ½ teaspoon of salt and crushed black pepper

Directions:

1. Preheat the grill to high heat and brush the grid with oil.

2. Combine all dry rub ingredients in a bowl. Rub the spice mixture on both sides of the meat and grill for 6 minutes on each side. Turn to cook the other side for 6 minutes and check internal temperature according to desired doneness.

3. Transfer on a wire rack, cover with foil and let it rest for 10 minutes before serving. Transfer to a serving platter and serve immediately.

BAKED SALMON AND ASPARAGUS IN FOIL

Preparation time: 15 minutes
Cooking time: 20 minutes
Serves: 4

Ingredients:

- 2 (6 oz.) wild caught salmon fillets
- 2 tablespoons grass fed ghee
- ½ teaspoon dried oregano
- Celtic or real salt and black pepper
- ½ pound of asparagus spears
- 1 large onion, sliced into rings
- 1 lemon, sliced into rounds
- 1 tablespoon of minced parsley

Directions:

1. Preheat the oven to a temperature of 400°F and cut 2 (12-inch) sheets of foil, set aside.

2. Lightly brush both sides of the fillets with ghee and season with oregano, salt and pepper on both sides.

3. Divide the asparagus into two portions and arrange properly on the center of the foil. Lay the fillet on top of the asparagus and place the onion and lemon on top. Fold both

sides of the foil and fold the bottom and top part to secure the ingredients.

4. Transfer to a baking sheet and bake it in the oven for 15 to 20 minutes. Remove the fish from the oven and let it rest for 10 minutes before removing the foil.

5. Divide asparagus to four serving plates, cut the fillets into halves and place it over the asparagus. Serve immediately with parsley on top.

HEALTHY HIGH FIBER HUMMUS

Preparation time: 5 minutes
Serves: 1 to 2

Ingredients:

- 1.5 cups of chickpeas (washed)
- 4 tablespoons of hulled tahini
- 1 clove of garlic, diced
- Juice from one medium sized lemon
- 1 teaspoon cumin powder
- Half a teaspoon of cinnamon powder
- 2 tablespoons of water
- 2 tablespoons of extra virgin olive oil
- One pinch of ground course sea salt, or to taste
- Black pepper to taste

Directions:

1. Simply use a food processor to thoroughly process all of the ingredients, then serve.

ARUGULA SALAD WITH CHICKEN AND APRICOTS

Preparation time: 15 minutes
Cooking time: 10 minutes
Serves: 4

Ingredients:

For the Chicken:

- 4 free range chicken breast fillets, slice into long and wide strips
- 1 tablespoon of fresh parsley leaves, minced
- 1 teaspoon dried tarragon leaves
- ¼ teaspoon crushed black pepper

For the Vinaigrette:

- 3 tablespoons of extra virgin olive oil
- 1 tablespoon white wine vinegar
- ½ teaspoon of salt
- 2 small pinches of ground black pepper

For the Salad:

- 4 cups packed fresh baby arugula
- 1 head green lettuce, leaves separated
- 1 cup sliced apricots

- ½ cup thinly sliced red onion

Directions:

1. Preheat the gas or charcoal grill to high heat, lightly brush the grids with oil and reduce heat to medium.

2. In a small mixing bowl, whisk together the vinegar, remaining salt and a pinch of black pepper. Mix in the oil and whisk until well combined. Set aside.

3. Place the chicken in a large bowl, season with tarragon, parsley, half the salt and black pepper and toss to evenly coat the chicken with seasonings. Grill the chicken for about 3 to 4 minutes on each side, turn to cook the other side for another 3 minutes and transfer to a plate. Cover with foil to keep it warm and set aside.

4. Combine all ingredients for the salad in a large mixing bowl, pour in the vinaigrette and gently toss to evenly coat the salad ingredients.

5. Portion the salad into individual serving bowls or plates, portion grilled chicken into 4 and place it over the salad. Serve immediately.

BALSAMIC CHICKEN WITH CAULIFLOWER

Preparation time: 15 minutes
Cooking time: 45 minutes
Serves: 4

Ingredients:

- 4 pounds free range chicken breast fillets, cut into thirds

- ½ pound cauliflower, core-removed and detach florets

- 2 tablespoons of minced fresh parsley leaves, for serving

For the Balsamic Marinade:

- 3 tablespoons of balsamic vinegar

- ¼ cup nama shoyu or coconut aminos

- 1 ½ teaspoons of minced garlic

- 2 tablespoons grass fed ghee or olive oil

- Salt and coarsely ground black pepper, to taste

Directions:

1. Add all ingredients for the balsamic marinade in a non-reactive bowl and stir until well combined. Add the chicken, toss to coat evenly with the marinade mixture and cover the bowl. Marinate the chicken in the refrigerator for 2 to 4 hours.

2. Preheat an oven to 400°F.

3. Remove the chicken from the marinade mixture, transfer to a baking pan and bake for about 35 minutes.

4. Add the cauliflower into the marinade mixture and toss to coat evenly with the marinade.

5. Remove pan from the oven, add the cauliflower and cover with foil. Return into the oven and bake for 10 minutes, or until the cauliflower is soft and tender.

6. Remove from pan, portion into individual serving plates and serve warm with parsley on top.

SPICE-RUBBED CHICKEN WITH AVOCADO SALSA

Preparation time: 15 minutes
Cooking time: 15 minutes
Serves: 4

Ingredients:

- 4 free range organic chicken breasts halves (boneless and skinless)
- 1 tablespoon of olive oil

For the Spice rub:

- ½ teaspoon ground cumin
- 1 teaspoon of chili powder
- 1 teaspoon of smoked paprika
- ½ teaspoon of garlic powder
- Salt and coarsely ground pepper, to taste

For the Avocado Salsa:

- 1 cup of diced red tomato
- 1 cup avocado, pitted and diced
- ½ cup diced cucumber
- ¼ cup diced onion
- ¼ cup minced cilantro

- 2 tablespoons lime juice
- Salt and pepper

Directions:

1. Combine together all spice rub ingredients in a large bowl and add the chicken. Rub the spice mixture evenly on all sides and set aside.

2. Mix together all ingredients for the avocado salsa in a separate bowl, season to taste with salt and pepper and toss to combine. Cover bowl and chill before serving.

3. In a medium skillet, apply medium-high heat and add the oil. Add and cook the chicken for 10 to 12 minutes while stirring occasionally, or until the meat is thoroughly cooked.

4. Portion the chicken on individual serving plates and serve with avocado salsa on top.

SPICY BEEF AND BOK CHOY

Preparation time: 15 minutes
Cooking time: 20 minutes
Serves: 4

Ingredients:

- 1 ½ pounds of grass fed lean beef sirloin, sliced into thin strips

- Salt and crushed peppercorns, to taste

- 1 medium head pak choi, blanched and chopped

- 1 cup thinly sliced onion

- 3 to 4 tablespoons of nama shoyu or coconut aminos

- 1-inch piece of fresh ginger root, minced

- 2 teaspoons of minced garlic

- 1 teaspoon of crushed red pepper flakes

- 1 tablespoon of melted coconut oil

Directions:

1. Place the beef in a large bowl, season to taste with salt and pepper and toss to combine. Set aside.

2. In a large skillet, apply medium-high heat and melt the coconut oil. Sauté the garlic, ginger and pepper flakes for 1 minute and stir in the beef. Sauté for 4 minutes, remove from the pan and transfer to a plate.

3. In the same skillet, sauté the onions for 2 minutes or until translucent and add in the pak choi. Cook until the pak choi is slightly wilted and return the beef. Stir in the nama shoyu, season to taste with salt and pepper and cook until the pak choi is wilted and the beef is cooked through.

4. Remove from pan and portion into individual serving plates. Serve immediately with extra pepper flakes on top if desired.

STEAK SALAD, THAI-STYLE

Preparation time: 15 minutes
Cooking time: 15 minutes
Serves: 4

Ingredients:

- 1 pound grass fed lean beef strip steaks
- ¼ cup Thai salad dressing
- ¼ cup chopped almonds
- ¼ cup minced fresh cilantro leaves
- ¼ cup minced fresh mint leaves

For the Marinade:

- Salt and crushed pepper, to taste
- ¼ cup nama shoyu or coconut aminos
- 1-inch piece of fresh ginger root, minced
- 2 teaspoons of minced garlic
- 1 Thai red chili pepper, chopped
- 1 organic lime, juiced

For the Salad:

- 2 cups of fresh red lettuce
- 2 cups of fresh green lettuce
- 1 red sweet pepper, sliced into strips

- ½ cucumber, sliced into thin rounds

Directions:

1. Mix all marinade ingredients in a bowl, add the beef and toss to coat the meat with marinade mixture. Cover and chill for 1 hour.

2. Preheat grill to medium-high heat and lightly brush the grids with oil. Grill the steaks for 5 minutes on each side, turn to cook the other side for 4 minutes more.

3. Transfer the steaks to a cutting board, let it rest for about 5 minutes and thinly slice across the grain.

4. Place all salad ingredients in a large bowl, drizzle with Thai dressing and gently toss to combine.

5. Divide into four serving plates and top with sliced steaks. Serve immediately with mint, almonds and cilantro on top.

SWEET POTATO POWERHOUSE MASH

Preparation time: 5 minutes
Cooking time: 30 minutes
Serves: 1

Ingredients:

- 1 sweet potato (wash but don't peel)

- 1 teaspoon of coconut oil

- 1 tablespoon of almond butter

- Ground course sea salt and freshly ground black pepper, to taste

Directions:

1. Preheat oven to 400 F.

2. Using a fork, puncture the sweet potato 4 to 5 times to prevent it from exploding.

3. Bake on a tray for approximately 30 minutes. It is done when you can easily slide a fork into and out of the sweet potato

4. Remove from oven (be careful it will be very hot!) then cut and scoop out the flesh into a bowl. Add the coconut oil and almond butter, season with the salt and pepper, mash, and serve.

BEEF STIR-FRY WITH ASPARAGUS

Preparation time: 15 minutes
Cooking time: 20 minutes
Serves: 4

Ingredients:

- 1 ½ pounds grass fed beef strip steaks, sliced into strips
- ½ pound of mushrooms, sliced
- Salt and ground pepper, to taste
- 1 teaspoon of crushed red pepper flakes
- 8 oz. trimmed asparagus
- ½ tablespoon olive oil

For the Sauce:

- ¼ cup of nama shoyu or coconut aminos
- 1 tablespoon of minced garlic
- 1-inch piece of fresh ginger root, minced
- 2 to 3 teaspoons of apple cider vinegar

Directions:

1. In pot with boiling water, blanch the asparagus for 3 to 4 minutes and remove from the pot. Transfer into a bowl with ice bath, cool and drain.

2. Combine all sauce ingredients in a bowl and mix until well combined. Cover and set aside.

3. In a medium non-stick skillet, apply medium heat and add the oil. Sauté the mushrooms for 4 minutes while stirring regularly, until lightly browned and tender. Remove from skillet, transfer to a plate and set aside.

4. In the same skillet, increase heat to high and fry the beef until evenly browned on all sides and cooked through. Reduce to medium heat, stir in the red pepper flakes and season to taste with salt and pepper.

5. Return mushroom in the skillet, add the asparagus and pour in sauce mixture. Cook until it reaches to a boil while stirring occasionally and remove from heat.

6. Divide into four serving plates and serve immediately.

WHOLE FOOD DINNER RECIPES

BEEF STIR-FRY WITH BAMBOO SHOOTS AND CABBAGE

Preparation time: 15 minutes
Cooking time: 25 minutes
Serves: 4

Ingredients:

- 2 pounds of ground grass-fed lean beef

- 1 medium head cabbage, shredded

- 1 cup of bamboo shoots, julienned

- 1-inch piece of fresh ginger root, julienned

- 2 teaspoons of minced garlic

- 1 cup of vegetable stock

- ¼ cup thinly sliced scallions

- 2 tablespoons of toasted sesame seeds

- ½ teaspoon of crushed black pepper

- 1 tablespoon of ghee

Directions:

1. In a pan over medium high heat, add the ground beef and cook for about 6 to 8 minutes or until lightly brown. Add

the 2 teaspoons of garlic, cook for 3 minutes and stir in the ginger and bamboo shoots. Season to taste with black pepper, pour in ½ cup of stock and add the sesame seeds. Cook for another 3 minutes while stirring regularly and remove from heat.

2. In a separate pan, apply medium-high heat and add the ghee. Add the cabbage, cover and cook until soft and wilted. Uncover and stir in 1 teaspoon of minced garlic, cook for 3 minutes while tossing occasionally and pour in ½ cup of stock. Cook until the stock has reduced in half and remove the pan from heat.

3. Portion the cabbage on individual serving plates and top each with the cooked ground beef and bamboo shoots mixture. Serve immediately.

SPICE-GRILLED LEMON SHRIMPS

Preparation time: 10 minutes
Cooking time: 8 to 10 minutes
Serves: 3 to 4

Ingredients:

- 1 pound peeled and deveined wild-caught shrimps

- 1 organic lemon, sliced into wedges

- 2 tablespoons minced parsley

- Olive oil, for greasing

For the Marinade:

- ¼ cup grass fed ghee

- 1 teaspoon of minced garlic

- 2 tablespoons of lemon juice

- ½ teaspoon of seasoned salt

- ½ teaspoon of black pepper

- 1 teaspoon mixed Italian herbs

Directions:

1. Combine all marinade ingredients in a medium bowl and whisk until well combined. Add the shrimp and coat evenly with the marinade mixture. Cover bowl and chill for 1 hour before cooking.

2. Preheat grill to high and brush the grids with oil.

3. Insert 2 to 3 shrimps on each skewer, brush with marinade and grill for 3 minutes on each side. Turn to cook the other side for 3 minutes more and transfer into a serving platter.

4. Serve warm with lemons wedges and sprinkle with minced parsley.

SEARED SCALLOPS WITH SAUTÉED KALE

Preparation time: 5 minutes
Cooking time: 10 minutes
Serves: 4

Ingredients:

- 1 pound large scallops

- 2 tablespoons of ghee

- 2 cups packed kale, chopped

- 1 large shallot, minced

- ½ cup of vegetable stock

- ½ tablespoon of apple cider vinegar

- Salt and black pepper, to taste

- ½ teaspoon smoked paprika

Directions:

1. Add 1 tablespoon of ghee in a skillet and apply with medium heat. Season the scallops with salt and pepper and pan-fry for 2 minutes on each side. Transfer to a plate and set aside.

2. In the same skillet, add the remaining ghee and sauté the shallots for 2 minutes and stir in the kale. Cook for 3 minutes while tossing regularly until the kale slightly

wilted. Add in the rest of the ingredients and cook until the stock has reduced in half.

3. Divide the sautéed kale in four serving plates and top with pan-seared scallops. Serve immediately.

GLAZED SALMON WITH ROASTED BROCCOLINI AND ASPARAGUS

Preparation time: 15 minutes
Cooking time: 20 minutes
Serves: 4 to 6

Ingredients:

- 4 (6 oz.) fresh wild Atlantic salmon fillets (boneless and skinless)

For the Marinade:

- ¼ cup of coconut aminos

- ½ teaspoon of ginger powder

- 2 garlic cloves, minced

- ½ teaspoon of Celtic or real salt

- ½ teaspoon of crushed black pepper

For the Vegetables:

- ½ pound of broccolini, trimmed

- ½ pound of asparagus, trimmed

- 2 tablespoons of ghee

- 1 tablespoon of organic lemon juice

- 3 crushed garlic cloves

- Salt and crushed black pepper, to taste

Directions:

1. Preheat the oven to 400°F, lightly grease a baking dish with ghee and set aside.

2. Combine together all marinade ingredients in a bowl and mix until well combined.

3. Place the fillets on the prepared baking dish and pour over marinade to fully cover the fillets. Set aside.

4. Add all ingredients for the vegetables in large bowl, gently toss to combine and transfer on a separate rimmed baking tray.

5. Roast fillets and vegetables for 15 to 20 minutes, or until the fish is done and the vegetables are tender.

6. Divide roasted vegetables on four serving plates, add the fish fillet on top and serve immediately.

FRESH SNAPPER CEVICHE

Preparation time: 15 minutes
Cooking time: 20 minutes
Serves: 2

Ingredients:

- Approximately 750g of fresh snapper, ensure all bones are removed and cut the meat into small cubes between 1 and 1.5 cm each

- Juice from three fresh, medium sized limes

- 1.5 cups of coconut water

- 2 tablespoons of coriander leaves, chopped

- 2 tablespoons of mint leaves, chopped

- 4 spring onions, sliced fine

- 1 small red chili, sliced fine

- Pinch of ground course sea salt

SALSA INGREDIENTS (if using as a dip)

- 1 ripe avocado, dice the flesh of the avocado into cubes of 1-2 cm each

- 1 red capsicum, diced

- 2 tablespoons chopped coriander

- Juice from half a lime (lime zest to taste)

Directions:

1. Mix herbs, chili, lime juice, coconut water, and spring onions, in small bowl.

2. Add fish to mix and ensure all cubes are thoroughly coated.

3. Cover and refrigerate for 3-5 hours.

4. Garnish with additional coriander and mint to taste. Serve on it's own or as a dip with your favorite vegetables, or shrimp if you want additional protein.

GREEK MEATBALLS WITH AVOCADO TZATZIKI SAUCE

Preparation time: 15 minutes
Cooking time: 25 minutes
Serves: 4

Ingredients:

For the Meatballs:

- 1 pound ground grass-fed beef
- 1 small red onion, minced
- 1 ½ teaspoons minced garlic
- 1 organic lemon, zested
- 1 teaspoon of dried oregano
- ½ teaspoon cumin powder
- ½ teaspoon of coriander powder
- Pink Himalayan salt and pepper, to taste

For the Sauce:

- 1 avocado, diced
- 1 cucumber, diced
- 1 teaspoon minced garlic
- 1 tablespoon minced red onion
- 1 lemon, juiced

- 2 teaspoons minced dill

- Salt and black pepper, to taste

Directions:

1. Preheat an oven to a temperature of 350°F. Lightly grease a baking pan with oil and set aside.

2. Combine all meatball ingredients until well combined and from into 2-inch balls. Transfer on the prepared baking pan and bake for 25 minutes, or until lightly browned and cooked through.

3. While cooking the meatballs, add all sauce ingredients in a food processor and pulse until smooth. Transfer to a bowl and set aside.

4. When the meatballs are done. Transfer into a serving platter and pour Tzatziki sauce over the meatballs. Serve immediately.

MEDITERRANEAN QUINOA PITAS

Preparation time: 15 minutes
Cooking time: 15 minutes
Serves: 4

Ingredients:

- 0.5 cup quinoa, washed

- 1 medium sized chopped carrot

- 5 scallions, sliced thin

- 2 cups of any white beans (i.e. navy beans), as always ensure your beans are thoroughly washed and inspected for rocks

- 0.25 cups of whole grain bread crumbs

- 1 egg, preferably from your local farmers market

- 2 tablespoons extra virgin olive oil

- Half an English cucumber, cut in diagonal thin slices

- Ground coarse sea salt to taste

- Dash of ground pepper, to taste

- 1 tablespoon ground cumin

- 0.5 cup of plain Greek yogurt

- 1 tablespoon fresh lemon juice

- 4 whole wheat pitas

Directions:

1. Cook quinoa according to instructions on package, then set aside.

2. Process carrot in your food processor until pieces are finely chopped, then add the cooked quinoa, egg, beans, breadcrumbs, cumin, 1 teaspoon of ground sea salt, a quarter of a teaspoon of pepper and half the scallions.

3. Process until the ingredients are mixed, but still chunky.

4. Spoon the mixture into four patties, then refrigerate for 15 minutes to firm them up if necessary.

5. Heat oil in a pan over medium heat, then brown the patties, 6-8 minutes per side.

6. Mix lemon juice, Greek yogurt, and the other half of the scallions; season with ground coarse sea salt and pepper to taste.

7. Portion the mixture into the pitas, add one of the patties to each pita and serve.

COCONUT CHICKEN SATAY

Preparation time: 15 minutes
Cooking time: 12 to 15 minutes
Serves: 4

Ingredients:

- 1 pound of free range chicken tenders
- ¼ cup unsweetened shredded coconut flakes

For the Sauce:

- ½ cup of tahini sauce
- ½ cup coconut milk
- 2 tablespoons fresh lime juice
- 1 ½ teaspoons minced garlic
- 1 jalapeno pepper, seeded and chopped
- ½ teaspoon crushed red pepper flakes

Directions:

1. Preheat an oven to high with a broiler setup and position the rack on the top. Line a baking sheet with foil and set aside.

2. Add all sauce ingredients in a food processor and pulse into a coarse mixture. Transfer to a bowl and set aside.

3. Insert 4 to 5 chicken strips on each skewer, brush with ¼ sauce mixture evenly on all areas and place it on the prepared baking sheet.

4. Place the baking sheet with chicken on the rack and broil for 6 minutes. Open the broiler and turn the skewers, brush with another remaining sauce. Broil for 6 minutes more and remove from the oven when cooked through.

5. Transfer on a serving platter and pour with the remaining sauce on top.

6. Sprinkle with toasted shredded coconut and serve warm.

RAWLICIOUS SPINACH STUFFED PORTOBELLO CAPS

Preparation time: 15 minutes

Serves: 4

Ingredients:

- 4 portobello mushroom caps

- Juice three fresh medium sized lemons and zest one teaspoon (or to taste)

- Half a cup of cashews

- 5 tablespoons of extra virgin olive oil

- 3 mined cloves of garlic

- 2 sliced scallions

- Pinch of ground course sea salt (or to taste)

- 2 teaspoons of fresh rosemary, chopped

- 1 cup of spinach leaves

- 1 cup of corn kernels

Directions:

1. Combine and whisk oil, rosemary, garlic, salt, lemon juice and zest.

2. Place the mushroom caps, rounded side facing down, in a baking dish. Gently pierce each cap several times with a fork or the tip of a knife.

3. Pour the mixture in equal portions in the mushroom caps, then cover and refrigerate between 3 and 8 hours.

4. Soak cashews in warm water for 20-40 minutes. Drain the water and process in your food processor with 0.25 cups of fresh water until you have a smooth puree. Add some ground course sea salt to taste.

5. Spoon the cashew puree into the mushroom caps. Garnish the mushroom caps with spinach, corn, scallions, and serve.

BAKED GARLIC CHICKEN WITH MUSHROOMS

Preparation time: 10 minutes
Cooking time: 30 minutes
Serves: 4

Ingredients:

- 1 ½ pounds of free range skinless chicken thighs
- ½ pound sliced Cremini mushrooms
- 1 cup homemade free range chicken stock or broth
- 1 medium head of garlic, crushed and peeled
- 2 tablespoons of ghee
- ½ teaspoon of onion powder
- ½ teaspoon of dried sage leaves
- ½ teaspoon of cayenne pepper
- ¼ teaspoon of crushed black pepper
- ¼ teaspoon of pink Himalayan salt

Directions:

1. Preheat an oven to a temperature of 375°F. Season chicken with salt and pepper and stead aside.

2. In an ovenproof pan, apply high heat and add 1 tablespoon of ghee. Once the ghee is hot, sear both sides of the chicken

for 3 minutes. Remove from the pan and transfer to plate and set aside.

3. Add the remaining ghee in the same pan and apply medium-high heat. Sauté the garlic until lightly brown and fragrant. Stir in the mushrooms, pour in the stock and cook until it reaches to a boil. Remove from pan, transfer to a plate and set aside.

4. Return chicken into the pan and spread the mushrooms evenly over the chicken. Season with salt and pepper and bake it in the oven for 15 minutes, or until the chicken is cooked through.

5. Remove the chicken and transfer to a serving platter. Transfer the mushrooms and all contents from the pan into a food processor and pulse until smooth and thick.

6. Pour the gravy on top of the chicken and serve immediately.

BAKED SALMON WITH AVOCADO SALSA

Preparation time: 10 minutes
Cooking time: 15 minutes
Serves: 4 to 6

Ingredients:

- 3 fillets of wild Atlantic salmon
- 1 tablespoon of onion powder
- 1 teaspoon of Spanish paprika
- 1 teaspoon of ground cumin
- Salt and crushed black pepper, to taste
- 2 tablespoons of ghee or olive oil

For the Salsa:

- 2 ripe avocados, pitted and diced
- ½ cup of minced onions
- 2 jalapeno peppers, seeded and minced
- 3 organic limes, juiced
- 2 tablespoons of extra virgin olive oil
- 2 tablespoons of minced fresh cilantro leaves
- Salt and crushed black pepper, to taste

Directions:

1. Combine all salsa ingredients in a large bowl and set aside. Cover the bowl with plastic wrap and chill before using.

2. Preheat the oven to a temperature of 400°F. Lightly grease a baking pan with oil and set aside.

3. Combine all spices in a small bowl and rub evenly on both sides of the salmon. Place the salmon on the prepared baking pan and drizzle with clarified butter on top of the salmon. Bake it in the oven for 15 minutes or until the fish flakes easily with a fork and cooked through. Remove from the oven and transfer on a serving plate.

4. Serve baked salmon warm with avocado salsa.

CREAMY BEEF PUMPKIN SOUP

Preparation time: 10 minutes
Cooking time: 45 minutes
Serves: 6

Ingredients:

- 2 tablespoons grass fed ghee

- 1 pound of ground grass fed beef

- 1 large red onion, julienned

- 2 green Jalapeno peppers, seeded and diced

- 2 large zucchini, cut into cubes

- 4 cups of homemade grass fed beef stock or broth

- 2 ½ cups of tomato sauce

- 2 cups of pumpkin puree

- 1 ½ teaspoons garlic powder

- 1 ½ teaspoons dried oregano

Directions:

1. Add 1 tablespoon of ghee in a large heavy bottomed pot and apply medium-high heat. Add the beef, cook for 6 minutes while stirring occasionally until lightly browned. Remove from pot and transfer into a bowl.

2. Add the remaining ghee in the pot and sauté the onions, peppers and zucchini for 5 minutes until the vegetables are soft and tender.

3. Add ¼ cup of stock and cook while scraping the browned bits on the bottom of the pan. Return the beef together with the remaining ingredients and bring to a boil. Reduce to low heat and simmer for 15 to 20 minutes, or until thick and creamy.

4. Remove from heat and portion the soup into six serving bowls. Sprinkle with extra oregano and serve warm.

SUPER SIMPLE CHICKPEA SALAD PITAS

Preparation time: 20 minutes

Serves: 2 to 4

Ingredients:

- 0.5 cups of chopped celery

- 1.5 cups of cooked chickpeas

- 1 medium sized dill pickle, chopped

- 1 garlic clove, minced

- 3 tablespoons of chopped red onion

- 1 tablespoon of fresh dill, minced

- 2 tablespoons of fresh lemon juice

- 0.5 cups of toasted sunflower seeds

- Course ground sea salt and pepper to taste

- 4 whole wheat pitas

Directions:

1. Preheat toaster oven to 325F and toast your sunflower seeds for 8-10 minutes.

2. Mix all of the ingredients into a bowl.

3. Spoon the mixture into some fresh whole wheat pitas and enjoy!

ROASTED GARLIC AND ARTICHOKE STUFFED CHICKEN

Preparation time: 15 minutes
Cooking time: 12 to 15 minutes
Serves: 6

Ingredients:

- 6 free range chicken breast fillets, butterfly cut

- 1 teaspoon poultry seasoning

- 1 cup loosely packed baby spinach, chopped

For the Stuffing:

- 8 garlic cloves, crushed and peeled

- 10 medium artichoke hearts

- 1 teaspoon of fleur de sel or salt

- ½ teaspoon black pepper

- ½ cup loosely packed parsley, finely chopped

- ¼ cup olive oil

Directions:

1. Preheat the grill to high and brush the grid with oil.

2. Add all stuffing ingredients in a food processor except for the oil and pulse into a coarse mixture. Pulse again while gradually adding the oil until smooth and well incorporated.

3. Divide the artichoke mixture into 6 portions and stuff into each butterflied breast together with the spinach.

4. Slowly fold one side of the fillet to cover the stuffing and secure the edge with soaked wooden skewer. Lightly brush both sides with oil and season with salt, pepper and poultry seasoning.

5. Grill the stuffed breast for 6 minutes on each side and turn to cook the other side for another 6 minutes. Check doneness and cook further until the meat is thoroughly cooked.

6. Transfer to a cutting board, let it rest for 5 minutes and slice into halves. Place it on a serving platter and serve with chopped parsley on top.

MILKFISH IN SOUR BROTH

Preparation time: 5 minutes
Cooking time: 30 minutes
Serves: 4

Ingredients:

- 1 large fresh milkfish, gills-removed and cut into serving pieces
- 2 tablespoons of tamarind pulp or Tamarind Seasoning Mix
- 1 cup of diced red tomatoes
- ½ cup of diced onion
- 8 pods of fresh okra, core-removed
- 1 cup packed water spinach, trimmed and chopped
- 4 jalapeno peppers, stems removed
- 4 cups of fish stock or water
- ¼ teaspoon of salt
- 1 stem of green onions, for serving

Directions:

1. Pour the stock into a large pot, apply high heat and bring it to a boil. Add the tomatoes, tamarind pulp/seasoning and onions and cook until it returns to a boil. Add the fish, simmer for 15 minutes and add in the rest of the ingredients.

2. Simmer for 5 minutes or until the spinach is lightly wilted. Remove pot from heat and let it rest for 5 minutes before serving.

3. Portion the fish and vegetable soup four serving bowls and serve with chopped green onions.

LEMON PEPPER KALE AND GARLIC SALMON

Preparation time: 10 minutes
Cooking time: 20 minutes
Serves: 1

Ingredients:

- 1 salmon fillet

- Half a bunch of fresh kale, chopped

- 1 red bell pepper, sliced

- 5 cloves of garlic, finely chopped

- Juice from one medium sized freshly squeezed lemon

- 1-2 tablespoons of almond butter

- Half a red onion, diced

- 3 tablespoons of lemon pepper (or to taste)

Directions:

1. In a non-stick pan, or a pan lightly coated extra virgin olive oil, fry the salmon fillet 3-5 minutes per side over medium heat.

2. With one minute left of cooking, add half the finely chopped garlic and lemon juice to the pan, then spoon over salmon fillet when serving.

3. Melt the almond butter in a pan over medium-low heat and add onion and red bell pepper.

4. After 3 minutes, add the chopped kale and the other half of the garlic. Sprinkle with lemon pepper.

5. Use tongs to turn and mix the kale with the other ingredients in the pan. Ensure the kale is heated evenly. Remove after only 2 minutes.

6. Serve and enjoy! For more lemon flavor, garnish the salmon fillet with a thin slice of lemon and sprinkle with lemon pepper.

SPICY COCONUT CHICKEN SOUP

Preparation time: 5 minutes
Cooking time: 40 minutes
Serves: 4

Ingredients:

- 1 cup of fresh coconut milk

- 1 pound of free range chicken breast fillet

- 1 chayote, peeled and sliced

- ½ cup of sliced red onion

- 2-inch piece of fresh ginger root, julienned

- 2 teaspoons minced garlic

- 1 cup free range chicken stock or broth

- 1 red sweet pepper, sliced into strips

- 1 hot green chili pepper, chopped

- 2 teaspoons coconut oil

- Salt and white pepper, to taste

Directions:

1. In a large stock pot, apply medium-high heat and add the oil. Sauté the onion, ginger and garlic for 3 minutes, or until lightly brown and aromatic. Add the chicken and red pepper and cook for 5 minutes while turning occasionally.

2. Add the chili pepper, sweet pepper and stock and cook until it reaches to a boil. Add in the coconut milk and chayote and season to taste with salt and pepper. Bring to a boil, reduce to low heat and simmer for 5 minutes and remove the pot from heat.

3. Divide into four serving bowls and serve with chopped green onions if desired.

4. Stir in the chili pepper and pour in the stock and coconut milk, bring to a boil. Season to taste with salt and pepper and reduce to low heat. Simmer for 30 minutes or until the sauce has thickened, add the chayote and cook further until the chicken is cooked through.

5. Remove pot from heat and leave for 10 minutes before serving on individual serving bowls.

CHICKEN ADOBO

Preparation time: 10 minutes
Cooking time: 35 minutes
Serves: 4

Ingredients:

- 1 ½ pound of free range chicken thighs and drumsticks

- ½ cup pineapple chunks

- 1 teaspoon ghee or olive oil

For the Marinade:

- ¼ cup raw cane vinegar

- ½ cup diced onion

- ½ cup nama shoyu or coconut aminos

- 4 garlic cloves, crushed

- 1 teaspoon of whole black peppercorns

- 2 to 3 dried laurel leaves

Directions:

1. In a container, combine together all marinade ingredients and add the chicken. Coat the chicken evenly with marinade mixture, cover the bowl and chill for at least for 2 hours. After marinating the chicken, drain and reserve the marinade.

2. Add the oil in a wok or pan and apply medium-heat. Fry the chicken for about 5 minutes while turning regularly, and add in the pineapple together with the marinade.

3. Bring to a boil, cover with lid and reduce to low heat. Simmer for 20 to 25 minutes until the chicken is tender and the sauce is thick.

4. Discard laurel leaf, transfer the chicken adobo to a serving bowl and serve immediately.

TOASTY KALE PECAN SQUASH

Preparation time: 20 minutes

Cooking time: 1 hour

Serves: 2 to 4

Ingredients:

- 1 medium sized butternut squash

- 3 garlic cloves, minced

- 4 tablespoons fresh parsley, chopped

- Pinch of ground course sea salt (or to taste)

- Half a tablespoon of extra virgin olive oil

- 1 cup of fresh chopped kale

ADDITIONAL INGREDIENTS TO BE PROCESSED:

- 1 tablespoon of nutritional yeast

- 0.25 cups of almonds

- 0.25 cups of pecans

- 1 teaspoon of extra virgin olive oil

- Pinch of ground course sea salt

Directions:

1. Preheat oven to 400F and lightly coat your casserole dish with oil.

2. Peel the squash, remove the top and bottom, then cut into two halves. Scoop out the guts and seeds. Further chop the two halves of squash into cubes of about 3 cm each and add the cubes to the casserole dish.

3. Add parsley, salt, minced garlic, and oil into the casserole dish and stir until well mixed with the squash cubes.

4. Cover and bake for 40-50 minutes.

5. While baking, combine the pecans, almonds, yeast, as well as a pinch of salt and 1 teaspoon of extra virgin olive oil in your food processor until chunky. Do not puree.

6. After 40-50 minutes, remove squash from the oven and turn off the heat. Add the chopped kale and sprinkle the mixture from the food processor all over the squash. Then return to the still hot oven for 5 minutes to warm the processed ingredients. Serve and enjoy!

GRILLED LEMON CHICKEN WITH ROSEMARY

Preparation time: 10 minutes
Cooking time: 20 minutes
Serves: 4

Ingredients:

- 2 whole free range chicken breasts, deboned and halved
- 1 lemon, cut into wedges
- Olive oil or ghee, for greasing

For the Marinade:

- 1 organic lemon, juiced and zested
- 2 tablespoons chopped fresh rosemary
- 1 teaspoon Italian seasoning mix
- 2 tablespoons of raw coconut aminos or nama shoyu
- 2 garlic cloves, minced
- ½ teaspoon fleur de set
- ½ teaspoon freshly ground black pepper

Directions:

1. In a large bowl, combine together all marinade ingredients and add the chicken. Coat the chicken evenly with the marinade mixture, cover bowl and chill for at least 2 hours.

2. Preheat the grill on high and lightly coat the grids with oil. Grill the chicken for 6 to 8 minutes per side, turn to cook the other side for 6 to 7 minutes or until the chicken is cooked through. While grilling the chicken, brush occasionally with the marinade mixture to add more flavor and aroma to the grilled chicken.

3. Check doneness and cook further if the center is not thoroughly cooked.

4. Place the grilled chicken on a serving plate and let it rest for 5 minutes before serving.

SOUTH OF THE BORDER SPICY PINTO BEANS

Preparation time: 15 minutes

Cooking time: 8 hours

Serves: 6 to 8 (or freeze extra servings)

Ingredients:

- 1 pound pinto beans, washed and inspected for rocks

- 2 cups of fresh diced tomatoes

- 6 diced green chili peppers

- 1 large chopped yellow onion

- 1 1/2 teaspoons garlic powder

- 1 tablespoon ground cumin

- 1 tablespoon chili powder

Directions:

1. Soak beans overnight in a bowl of water, fully immersed.

2. Place the drained beans in your crock pot, add fresh water such that all the beans are immersed, then add the onion, tomatoes, cumin, chili powder, and garlic powder.

3. Cook on high for 7-8 hours.

4. Serve alone or in a whole wheat pita

PAN-FRIED CHICKEN IN MUSHROOM SAUCE

Preparation time: 10 minutes
Cooking time: 1 hour
Serves: 4

Ingredients:

- 1 tablespoon of extra virgin olive oil
- 4 large, free-range chicken thigh (meat only)
- 1 cup homemade chicken stock
- 2 tablespoons of grass fed butter
- 1 cup sliced red onion
- ½ pound raw shiitake mushrooms
- ½ cup dry white wine or apple cider vinegar
- ¼ cup coconut cream
- 1 tablespoon of arrowroot starch
- Salt and black pepper, to taste

Directions:

1. Season the chicken with salt and black pepper on both sides and set aside.

2. Melt the butter in a non-stick pan over medium-high heat and add the chicken. Fry the chicken skin-side down for

about 10 minutes, or until golden brown. Transfer into a casserole dish and set aside.

3. In the same pan, sauté the onions for 2 to 3 minutes and stir in the mushrooms. Cook until the mushroom is soft and tender and pour in the wine/vinegar and stock. Bring to a boil while scraping the browned bits on the bottom of the pan.

4. Add into the casserole dish together with the cream and arrowroot starch. Mix to combine and bring it to a boil. Season to taste with salt and pepper, reduce to low heat and simmer for 30 minutes.

5. When the chicken is thoroughly cooked and the sauce has thickened, remove from heat and set aside to cool.

6. Serve warm in the casserole or transfer into a serving bowl.

Duck Breast Red Curry with Pineapples

Preparation time: 20 minutes
Cooking time: 2 hours
Serves 6

Ingredients:

- 4 free range skinless duck breast fillets
- ¼ cup fresh pineapple juice
- 3 to 4 tablespoons of Thai red curry paste or 2 tablespoons of curry powder
- 1 cup of fresh coconut milk
- 2 tablespoons of nama shoyu or coconut aminos
- 1 organic lime, juiced and zested
- 1 cup fresh pineapple, cut into chunks
- Salt and black pepper, to taste
- 1 red chili, deseeded and finely sliced, for serving
- ¼ cup fresh Thai basil leaves, for serving

Directions:

1. Preheat the oven to 350°F.
2. Season the breast with salt and pepper on both sides, set aside.

3. In an ovenproof skillet over medium-low heat, pan-fry the duck breast skin-side down for 10 to 15 minutes or until the meat has released most of its oil. Turn to cook the other side for 5 minutes, transfer to a plate and set aside.

4. In the same skillet, add the pineapple juice and curry paste cook until it starts boil. Pour in the coconut milk and ½ cup of water, bring to a boil. Reduce to low heat and add in nama shoyu, juice of lime, lime zest and duck breast. Stir to coat the meat evenly with sauce.

5. Cover the skillet and bake it in the oven for 1 hour 30 minutes. Remove from the oven and return into the stove. Stir in the pineapple, season to taste with salt and pepper and cook for 2 to 3 minutes.

6. Transfer into a serving platter and serve warm with sliced chilis and fresh basil on top.

Vegan Tofu Tacos

Preparation time: 15 minutes
Cooking time: 15 minutes
Serves: 2 to 4

Ingredients:

- 1 cup of cooked black beans

- 8 ounces of firm tofu

- Half a medium sized red onion, diced

- 1 cup fresh cilantro, chopped

- 1 or 2 sliced avocados

- 0.25 cup of pomegranate seeds

- Half a cup of salsa

- Corn tortillas

SEASONING FOR TOFU:

- Half a teaspoon of chili powder

- 1 teaspoon of cumin

- 1 teaspoon of garlic powder

- Pinch of ground course sea salt

- 1 tablespoon of salsa

- 1 tablespoon of water

Directions:

1. Wrap tofu in a clean, absorbent towel and place something heavy on top, such as a cast iron skillet, while prepping toppings.

2. Cook black beans according to instructions on package, add a pinch each of salt, chili powder, cumin, and garlic powder, then set aside.

3. Add the tofu seasoning and salsa to a bowl and top with just enough water to make a sauce that can be poured, then set aside.

4. Heat a pan over medium heat and add 1-2 tablespoons of oil and chopped tofu. Cook for 5 minutes, stirring frequently, then add seasoning. Cook for another 8 minutes, still stirring frequently.

5. Warm the tortillas and fill them with all of the ingredients, then serve and enjoy!

BEEF AND VEGETABLE CASSEROLE

Preparation time: 15 minutes
Cooking time: 2 to 2 ½ hours
Serves: 4

Ingredients:

- 1 ½ pounds stewing beef, cut into large cubes

- 2 medium stalks of celery, diced

- 1 cup diced onion

- 1 cup sliced carrots

- 3 bay leaves

- 2 ounces of thyme sprigs

- 1 tablespoon of olive oil

- 1 tablespoon grass fed butter

- 2 tablespoons of almond flour

- 2 tablespoons tomato sauce or purée

- 2 tablespoons of Worcestershire sauce

- 1 beef broth cube

- 1 ½ cup of homemade beef stock, hot

- Salt and black pepper, to taste

Directions:

1. Preheat the oven to 350°F.

2. In a casserole, place the carrots, onion, celery, thyme sprig, 1 tablespoon of oil and butter. Apply medium heat and cook for about 8 to 10 minutes or until soft and tender. Gradually mix in the flour and stir in the Worcestershire sauce, tomato sauce, bay leaf and beef cubes. Gradually pour the stock and stir in the beef.

3. Stir to combine, cover and bake it in the oven for 1 ½ hours. Uncover and cook for 30 minutes more, or until the meat is tender and cooked through.

4. When the beef is done and the sauce has thickened, remove from the oven and let it rest for about 10 minutes before serving.

5. Serve warm straight from the casserole.

VEGAN CHICKPEA SALAD

Preparation time: 15 minutes

Serves: 2 to 4

Ingredients:

- 3 cups cooked chickpeas

- Half a cup of chopped sun dried tomatoes

- 3 tablespoons fresh squeezed lemon juice

- 15 fresh basil leaves, chopped

- 1 tablespoon of apple cider vinegar

- 2 tablespoons of extra virgin olive oil

- Pinch of fresh ground pepper, to taste

Directions:

1. Blanch your sun dried tomatoes by placing them in a small bowl and pouring boiling fresh water over them, and soaking them for 5 minutes.

2. Drain the bowl, then slice the sun dried tomatoes.

3. Combine all ingredients including the sun dried tomatoes, serve and enjoy!

TURKEY BREAST WITH CITRUS SAUCE

Preparation time: 15 minutes
Cooking time: 2 hours
Serves: 4

Ingredients:

- 2 tablespoons of ghee/clarified grass fed butter

- 1 whole free range organic turkey breast

- Salt and coarsely ground black pepper

- 1 cup of homemade chicken stock

- 2 tablespoons of apple cider vinegar

- 1 orange, juiced and zested

- 1 teaspoon of cayenne pepper

Directions:

1. Generously season the turkey breast with salt and ground black pepper evenly on both sides. Set aside.

2. In a Dutch oven, apply medium-high heat and add 1 tablespoon of clarified butter. Brown the turkey breast evenly on both sides and transfer to a plate.

3. In the Dutch oven, add the remaining ghee together with the cider vinegar, orange juice and zest, cayenne and stock. Apply medium-high heat, bring to a boil while stirring occasionally and reduce to low heat.

4. Add the turkey breast, baste evenly with sauce and simmer for 1 ½ hour to 2 hours with lid. Cook until the meat is tender and cooked thoroughly.

5. If the meat is not yet tender, cook further until the desired doneness is achieved.

6. Transfer to plate, tent with foil and let it rest while preparing the sauce.

7. Simmer the sauce until it has reduced in half and has thickened and transfer to a bowl.

8. Carve the turkey breast and cut into thin slices. Transfer to a serving platter, drizzle with sauce on top and serve warm.

CRACKED PEPPER QUINOA SALMON CAKES

Preparation time: 15 minutes
Cooking time: 10 minutes
Serves: 3 to 4

Ingredients:

- 2 cups of fresh salmon, cooked and chopped into cubes of 1-2cm each

- 1 egg, preferably from you local farmer's market

- Half a cup of quinoa flakes (or substitute for any variety of fast cooking oats)

- 1 tablespoon low sodium soy sauce

- 2 cloves of garlic, minced

- 0.25 cups of fresh chopped parsley

- 2 teaspoons of freshly ground pepper, or to taste

- 1 tablespoon extra virgin coconut oil

- 2 green onions, thinly sliced

Directions:

1. Combine all ingredients other than the oil and mix in a bowl.

2. Spoon the mixture into patties (makes 6-8 patties).

3. Pour the oil in a medium sized pan and heat over medium-low heat.

4. Cook the salmon patties until golden brown, approximately 4 minutes per side.

5. Serve alone or in a warmed whole wheat pita with chopped romaine lettuce.

THAI PANANG BEEF CURRY

Preparation time: 15 minutes
Cooking time: 2 hours
Serves: 4 to 6

Ingredients:

- 1 ½ pounds of grass fed beef chuck steak, sliced into thin strips
- 2 tablespoons of olive oil
- 3 kaffir lime double leaves, cut into chiffonade (optional)
- 1 cup of coconut milk
- 2 tablespoons of nama shoyu or coconut aminos

For the Panang Curry Paste:

- 2 tablespoon of olive oil
- 1 tablespoon of water
- 2 tablespoons of red pepper flakes
- 1 teaspoon coriander seeds, grounded
- 1 teaspoon cumin seeds, grounded
- 1 teaspoon of salt
- 1-inch piece of fresh ginger root, minced
- 1 stalk of lemongrass (white part only), finely chopped
- 1 sprig of fresh cilantro leaves, chopped

- 1 shallot, quartered

- 2 garlic cloves, crushed

Directions:

1. Add all ingredients for the curry paste in a food processor and process the ingredients into a smooth mixture. Transfer to a bowl and set aside.

2. In a pan, apply medium-high heat and add the oil. Fry the kaffir lime leaves for 1 minute and stir in the curry paste. Reduce to low heat, cook for 2 to 3 minutes while stirring regularly.

3. Transfer into a large heavy bottomed pot and add the beef. Stir in the nama shoyu and coconut milk and toss to coat the beef with the sauce mixture.

4. Cover and cook on low heat for 2 to 3 hours, or until tender and cooked through. Adjust seasonings according to desired taste and remove the pot from heat.

5. Divide into four or six serving bowls and serve immediately.

Sesame Beef and Broccoli

Preparation time: 10 minutes
Cooking time: 2 to 2 ½ hours
Serves: 4 to 6

Ingredients:

- 1 ½ pounds of grass fed beef chuck steak, sliced into thin strips

- 1 medium head of broccoli, detached florets

- 2 tablespoons of arrow root starch

- ¼ cup organic beef stock or broth

- Toasted sesame seeds, for serving

For the Sauce

- 2 tablespoon of sesame oil

- ½ teaspoon of freshly ground black pepper

- ½ teaspoon of salt

- 1 cup of organic beef broth

- ½ cup of oyster sauce

Directions:

1. Combine together all sauce ingredients in a large heavy bottomed pot and add the beef. Toss to coat the beef evenly with the sauce mixture.

2. Cover pot, apply medium-high heat and cook until it reaches to a boil. Reduce to low heat and simmer 2 hours, or until the meat is tender and cooked through.

3. Before serving the beef, blanch the broccoli in a separate pot with boiling water for 2 to 3 minutes. Immediately transfer into a bowl with ice bath to stop further cooking, drain and set aside.

4. When the beef is done, combine together the starch and stock in a small bowl and add into the pot. Cook on high for 5 minutes or until it returns to a simmer and the sauce has thickened.

5. Stir in the broccoli, divide into six serving bowls and serve with toasted sesame seeds on top.

TOMATO GARLIC KALE SALAD

Preparation time:15 minutes
Serves: 1-2

Ingredients:

- Five sun-dried tomatoes

- A handful of finely chopped kale

- A handful of finely chopped spinach

- 1 Tbsp pumpkin seeds

- ¼ small, red onion

- One garlic clove

For the dressing:

- 1 tsp apple cider vinegar

- 1 Tbsp cold pressed oil

- A dash of garlic powder, pepper and chili

- ¼ tsp salt

For the toppings:

- fresh herbs and cherry tomatoes

Directions:

1. Place spinach and kale in a bowl and mix the dressing ingredients in another bowl.

2. Pour the dressing over the greens then chop the tomatoes, red onion and garlic clove. Add them to the greens and sprinkle pumpkin seeds on top.

3. Mix until well-combined and serve topped with cherry tomatoes and fresh herbs.

GRILLED CHICKEN AND SEASONED POTATOES

Preparation time:15 minutes
Cooking time: 20 minutes
Serves: 4

Ingredients:

For the Potato:

- 2 medium potatoes, quartered
- 1 tablespoon of extra virgin olive oil
- ½ teaspoon of smoked paprika
- ½ teaspoon of ground cinnamon
- A pinch of salt
- A pinch of crushed black pepper

For the Chicken:

- 4 boneless skinless chicken breasts
- ½ tablespoon of smoked paprika
- Salt and crushed black pepper

Directions:

1. In a bowl, add the potatoes and sprinkle with dry ingredients. Add the oil and gently toss to distribute the seasonings.

2. Season chicken with paprika, salt and pepper on both sides and set aside.

3. Preheat gas grill to medium-high heat and brush the grill with oil.

4. Grill potatoes on one side of the grill and the chicken on the other side.

5. Grill the potatoes for 10 minutes on each side and turn to cook the other side for 10 minutes. Grill the chicken for 6 to 8 minutes on each side, turn to cook the other side for another 6 minutes or until cooked through.

6. Place the chicken and potatoes on a serving platter and serve.

GRILLED CITRUS SALMON

Preparation time: 15 minutes
Cooking time: 15 minutes
Serves: 2

Ingredients:

- 2 salmon fillets

For the Marinade:

- 2 tablespoons of olive oil

- 1 lemon, juiced

- 1 lime, juiced

- 2 teaspoons of minced garlic

- 1 medium onion, minced

- 1 teaspoon black peppercorns, crushed

Directions:

1. Add all marinade ingredients in mixing bowl and whisk until well combined. Add salmon, coat evenly with marinade and let it stand for about 1 to 2 hours.

2. Preheat grill to high and lightly brush the grill with oil.

3. Reduce to medium heat and grill the salmon for about 6 to 8 minutes on each side. Turn to cook the other side and occasionally brush with marinade mixture while grilling.

4. When the salmon is done, transfer to a plate and serve.

SLICED CHICKEN BURRITO

Preparation time: 10 minutes
Cooking time: 15 minutes
Serves: 4

Ingredients:

- 1 pound of sliced chicken breasts
- 1 tablespoon of taco seasoning
- 1 teaspoon poultry seasoning
- Salt and black pepper, to taste
- 1 tablespoons grass fed ghee
- 4 gluten-free flour tortillas
- 1 red sweet pepper, minced
- 1 medium white onion, minced
- 1 stem green onions, chopped
- 2 tablespoons of salsa
- 1 ripe tomato, sliced
- 1 ripe avocado, sliced

Directions:

1. Add the sliced chicken, taco and poultry seasoning in a bowl. Season to taste with salt and pepper and mix until well combined.

2. Add the ghee in a medium skillet and apply medium-high heat. Cook the sliced chicken until until white and cooked through. Remove from skillet and add the sweet pepper, white onion and green onions in the same skillet, sauté for about 5 minutes. Remove from pan, transfer to the bowl with the sliced chicken and mix until well combined.

3. In the same pan, heat the tortillas for 1 minute on each side and place it on a flat work surface.

4. Divide the meat mixture, salsa, tomato and avocado on each tortilla and roll up to form into burritos. Slice into halves, transfer to a serving plate and serve immediately.

SHREDDED PORK AND MUSHROOM WITH GINGER SAUCE

Preparation time: 15 minutes
Cooking time: 20 minutes
Serves: 4

Ingredients:

- 1 ½ pounds shredded lean pork
- ½ pound of mushrooms, sliced
- Salt and ground pepper, to taste
- 1 teaspoon of crushed red pepper flakes
- 8 oz. trimmed asparagus
- ½ tablespoon olive oil

For the Sauce:

- ¼ cup of nama shoyu or coconut aminos
- 1 tablespoon of minced garlic
- 1-inch piece of fresh ginger root, minced
- 2 to 3 teaspoons of apple cider vinegar

Directions:

1. In pot with boiling water, blanch the asparagus for 3 to 4 minutes and remove from the pot. Transfer into a bowl with ice bath, cool and drain.

2. Combine all sauce ingredients in a bowl and mix until well combined. Cover and set aside.

3. In a medium non-stick skillet, apply medium heat and add the oil. Sauté the mushrooms for 4 minutes while stirring regularly, until lightly browned and tender. Remove from skillet, transfer to a plate and set aside.

4. In the same skillet, increase heat to high and fry the pork until evenly browned on all sides and cooked through. Reduce to medium heat, stir in the red pepper flakes and season to taste with salt and pepper.

5. Return mushroom in the skillet, add the asparagus and pour in sauce mixture. Cook until it reaches to a boil while stirring occasionally and remove from heat.

6. Divide into four serving plates and serve immediately.

GARLIC COD WITH ROASTED VEGETABLES

Preparation time: 15 minutes
Cooking time: 20 minutes
Serves: 4 to 6

Ingredients:

- 4 (6 oz.) fresh cod fillets (boneless and skinless)

For the Marinade:

- ¼ cup of coconut aminos
- ½ teaspoon of ginger powder
- 2 garlic cloves, minced
- ½ teaspoon of Celtic or real salt
- ½ teaspoon of crushed black pepper

For the Vegetables:

- ½ pound of broccoli florets, trimmed
- ½ pound of asparagus, trimmed
- 2 tablespoons of ghee
- 1 tablespoon of organic lemon juice
- 3 crushed garlic cloves
- Salt and crushed black pepper, to taste

Directions:

1. Preheat the oven to 400°F, lightly grease a baking dish with ghee and set aside.

2. Combine together all marinade ingredients in a bowl and mix until well combined.

3. Place the fillets on the prepared baking dish and pour over marinade to fully cover the fillets. Set aside.

4. Add all ingredients for the vegetables in large bowl, gently toss to combine and transfer on a separate rimmed baking tray.

5. Roast fillets and vegetables for 15 to 20 minutes, or until the fish is done and the vegetables are tender.

6. Divide roasted vegetables on four serving plates, add the fish fillet on top and serve immediately.

Lean Fried Pork Chops in Mushroom Sauce

Preparation time: 10 minutes
Cooking time: 1 hour
Serves: 4

Ingredients:

- 1 tablespoon of extra virgin olive oil

- 4 lean pork chops

- 2 tablespoons of grass fed butter

- 1 cup sliced red onion

- ½ pound raw shiitake mushrooms

- ½ cup dry white wine or apple cider vinegar

- ¼ cup coconut cream

- 1 tablespoon of arrowroot starch

- Salt and black pepper, to taste

Directions:

1. Season the pork chops with salt and black pepper on both sides and set aside.

2. Melt the butter in a non-stick pan over medium-high heat and add the pork chops. Fry the pork for about 4 to 6 minutes per side. Transfer into a casserole dish and set aside.

3. In the same pan, sauté the onions for 2 to 3 minutes and stir in the mushrooms. Cook until the mushroom is soft and tender and pour in the wine/vinegar. Bring to a boil while scraping the browned bits on the bottom of the pan.

4. Add into the casserole dish together with the cream and arrowroot starch. Mix to combine and bring it to a boil. Season to taste with salt and pepper, reduce to low heat and simmer for 30 minutes.

5. When the pork is thoroughly cooked and the sauce has thickened, remove from heat and set aside to cool.

6. Serve warm in the casserole or transfer into a serving bowl.

SEASONED TILAPIA WITH GREEN SAUCE

Preparation time: 10 minutes
Cooking time: 15 minutes
Serves: 4 to 6

Ingredients:

- 4 Tilapia fillets
- 1 tablespoon of onion powder
- 1 teaspoon of Spanish paprika
- 1 teaspoon of ground cumin
- Salt and crushed black pepper, to taste
- 2 tablespoons of ghee or olive oil

For the sauce:

- 2 ripe avocados, pitted and diced
- ½ cup of minced onions
- 2 jalapeno peppers, seeded and minced
- 3 organic limes, juiced
- 2 tablespoons of extra virgin olive oil
- 2 tablespoons of minced fresh cilantro leaves
- Salt and crushed black pepper, to taste

Directions:

1. Combine all sauce ingredients in a large bowl and set aside. Cover the bowl with plastic wrap and chill before using.

2. Preheat the oven to a temperature of 400°F. Lightly grease a baking pan with oil and set aside.

3. Combine all spices in a small bowl and rub evenly on both sides of the tilapia. Place the tilapia on the prepared baking pan and drizzle with clarified butter on top of the tilapia. Bake it in the oven for 15 minutes or until the fish flakes easily with a fork and is cooked through. Remove from the oven and transfer to a serving plate.

4. Serve baked tilapia warm with green sauce.

LEMON GRILLED SALMON WITH ITALIAN SEASONING

Preparation time: 10 minutes
Cooking time: 20 minutes
Serves: 4

Ingredients:

- 4 fresh Atlantic salmon fillets
- 1 lemon, cut into wedges
- Olive oil or ghee, for greasing

For the Marinade:

- 1 organic lemon, juiced and zested
- 2 tablespoons chopped fresh rosemary
- 1 teaspoon Italian seasoning mix
- 2 tablespoons of raw coconut aminos or nama shoyu
- 2 garlic cloves, minced
- ½ teaspoon fleur de set
- ½ teaspoon freshly ground black pepper

Directions:

1. In a large bowl, combine together all marinade ingredients and add the fish. Coat the fish evenly with the marinade mixture, cover bowl and chill for at least 2 hours.

2. Preheat the grill on high and lightly coat the grill with oil. Grill the fish for 6 to 8 minutes per side, or until the fish is cooked through. While grilling the fish, brush occasionally with the marinade mixture to add more flavor and aroma to the grilled fish.

3. Place the grilled fish on a serving plate and serve.

CHICKEN WITH ONIONS AND SHIITAKE MUSHROOMS

Preparation time: 10 minutes
Cooking time: 30 to 40 minutes
Serves: 4

Ingredients:

- 1 pound boneless skinless chicken breasts, cut into large cubes
- 2 tablespoons of olive oil
- Salt and black pepper, to taste
- 2 cups of fresh shiitake mushrooms
- 2 cups of chicken stock
- 1 medium white onion, sliced into rings
- 1 tablespoon minced garlic

Directions:

1. Season the chicken with salt and pepper and toss to coat it evenly with spices.

2. In a pot over medium-high heat, add the oil and cook chicken evenly on all sides until meat is white. Stir in the garlic and onions, sauté for 2 minutes and add the mushrooms

3. Season the chicken with salt and pepper on all sides. Stir in the onions and garlic and sauté for about 1 minute and then

add the mushrooms and the stock. Cover with lid, bring it to a boil and reduce to low heat. Simmer for about 15 minutes or until the meat is tender and cooked through.

4. Adjust the seasoning and transfer into a serving bowl. Serve immediately.

Join Albert Pino's VIP Club

Get access to exclusive content from Albert including healthy living tips, tricks and hacks, special discounts, recipes, and free books!

www.albertpino.com

54711815R00120

Made in the USA
Lexington, KY
25 August 2016